Biography Today

Profiles of People of Interest to Young Readers

Volume 19
Issue 3
September 2010

Cherie D. Abbey
Managing Editor

P.O. Box 31-1640
Detroit, MI 48231-1640

Cherie D. Abbey, *Managing Editor*

Peggy Daniels, Joan Goldsworthy, Jeff Hill, Kevin Hillstrom, Laurie Hillstrom, Justin Karr, Leslie Karr, and Diane Telgen, *Sketch Writers*

Allison A. Beckett and Mary Butler, *Research Staff*

* * *

Peter E. Ruffner, *Publisher*
Matthew P. Barbour, *Senior Vice President*

* * *

Elizabeth Collins, *Research and Permissions Coordinator*
Kevin M. Hayes, *Operations Manager*
Cherry Stockdale, *Permissions Assistant*

Shirley Amore, Martha Johns, and Kirk Kauffmann, *Administrative Staff*

Special thanks to Frederick G. Ruffner for creating this series.

Copyright © 2010 EBSCO Publishing, Inc.
ISSN 1058-2347 • ISBN 978-0-7808-1060-0

Library of Congress Cataloging-in-Publication Data

The information in this publication was compiled from sources cited and from sources considered reliable. While every possible effort has been made to ensure reliability, the publisher will not assume liability for damages caused by inaccuracies in the data, and makes no warranty, express or implied, on the accuracy of the information contained herein.

∞

This book is printed on acid-free paper meeting the ANSI Z39.48 Standard. The infinity symbol that appears above indicates that the paper in this book meets that standard.

Printed in the United States of America

Contents

Preface

Biography Today is a magazine designed and written for the young reader—ages 9 and above—and covers individuals that librarians and teachers tell us that young people want to know about most: entertainers, athletes, writers, illustrators, cartoonists, and political leaders.

The Plan of the Work

The publication was especially created to appeal to young readers in a format they can enjoy reading and readily understand. Each issue contains approximately 10 sketches arranged alphabetically. Each entry provides at least one picture of the individual profiled, and bold-faced rubrics lead the reader to information on birth, youth, early memories, education, first jobs, marriage and family, career highlights, memorable experiences, hobbies, and honors and awards. Each of the entries ends with a list of easily accessible sources designed to lead the student to further reading on the individual and a current address. Retrospective entries are also included, written to provide a perspective on the individual's entire career.

Biographies are prepared by Omnigraphics editors after extensive research, utilizing the most current materials available. Those sources that are generally available to students appear in the list of further reading at the end of the sketch.

Indexes

Cumulative indexes are an important component of *Biography Today*. Each issue of the *Biography Today* General Series includes a Cumulative Names Index, which comprises all individuals profiled in *Biography Today* since the series began in 1992. In addition, we compile three other indexes: the Cumulative General Index, Places of Birth Index, and Birthday Index. See our web site, www.biographytoday.com, for these three indexes, along with the Names Index. All *Biography Today* indexes are cumulative, including all individuals profiled in both the General Series and the Subject Series.

Our Advisors

This series was reviewed by an Advisory Board comprising librarians, children's literature specialists, and reading instructors to ensure that the concept of this publication—to provide a readable and accessible biographical magazine for young readers—was on target. They evaluated the title as it developed, and their suggestions have proved invaluable. Any errors, however, are ours alone. We'd like to list the Advisory Board members, and to thank them for their efforts.

Our Advisory Board stressed to us that we should not shy away from controversial or unconventional people in our profiles, and we have tried to follow their advice. The Advisory Board also mentioned that the sketches might be useful in reluctant reader and adult literacy programs, and we would value any comments librarians might have about the suitability of our magazine for those purposes.

Your Comments Are Welcome

Our goal is to be accurate and up-to-date, to give young readers information they can learn from and enjoy. Now we want to know what you think. Take a look at this issue of *Biography Today*, on approval. Write or call me with your comments. We want to provide an excellent source of biographical information for young people. Let us know how you think we're doing.

Cherie Abbey
Managing Editor, *Biography Today*
Omnigraphics, Inc.
P.O. Box 31-1640
Detroit, MI 48231-1640
800-234-1340
www.omnigraphics.com
editor@biographytoday.com

Congratulations!

Congratulations to the following individuals and libraries who are receiving a free copy of *Biography Today*, Vol. 19, No. 3, for suggesting people who appear in this issue.

Paul Bishette, Silas Bronson Library, Waterbury, CT

Ashley Daly, Ardmore High School, Ardmore, AL

Cierra Huggins, Toledo, OH

Kimberly Lentz, North Rowan High School, Spencer, NC

Ricza Lopez, Bronx, NY

Michelle D. Lyons, Jennings High School Library, Jennings, LA

Laurie Martucci-Walsh, McKenna Elementary School, Massapequa, NY

Jennifer McGuire, Esther Dennis Middle School, Dayton, OH

S.A. Schene, Homecroft Elementary, Indianapolis, IN

Laurie Skien, Bushnell-Prairie City Jr. High School, Bushnell, IL

Shreya Subramanian, Martell Elementary School, Troy, MI

Owen V., McKenna Elementary School, Massapequa, NY

Justin Bieber 1994-

Canadian Musician
Creator of the Hit Albums *My World* and *My World 2.0*

BIRTH

Justin Bieber was born on March 1, 1994, in Stratford, Ontario, Canada. His parents broke up when he was 10 months old. His father, Jeremy, eventually moved to Winnipeg, Manitoba, where he works in construction. He has kept up a relationship with his son, but Bieber has been raised by his mother, Pattie Mallette. She eventually remarried, and Bieber now has two younger half-siblings.

YOUTH

Bieber's mother was 19 years old when he was born. She had dreamed of becoming an actress, but as a young, single parent, she found she had to work more than one job just to support herself and her baby. She designed web sites, did office work, and played music for a church group. Her parents lived nearby, and they helped her out, but it was still very difficult. "We were living below the poverty line," she recalled. "We had a roof over our heads and we had food in the house, but we really struggled."

—————— " ——————

"I've always loved music, especially percussion," Bieber said. "My mom bought me my first drum kit when I was four because I was banging on everything around the house, even couches. I picked up the guitar when I was six and taught myself to play, but I didn't really start singing until I was 10."

—————— " ——————

Although she didn't have much money, Mallette did whatever she could to encourage her young son to develop his talent, which was obvious even when he was very young. "I've always loved music, especially percussion," Bieber said. "My mom bought me my first drum kit when I was four because I was banging on everything around the house, even couches. I picked up the guitar when I was six and taught myself to play, but I didn't really start singing until I was 10." He also taught himself to play keyboards and the trumpet. "When he was five, he'd hear something on the radio and go to the keyboard and figure it out," his mother remembered. He liked to sing, too, though he was more focused on instrumental music at first.

EDUCATION

Bieber attended the Stratford Northwestern Secondary School, where he played hockey and soccer. Since his singing career has taken off, he has a private tutor who makes sure that he gets at least 15 hours a week of class time. He also has voice lessons on a regular basis.

CAREER HIGHLIGHTS

When Bieber was 12 years old, he entered a local talent competition. Styled after the popular television program "American Idol," it was called "Stratford Idol." "The other people in the competition had been taking singing lessons and had vocal coaches. I wasn't taking it too seriously at the time," he recalled. "I would just sing around the house." Despite his relaxed approach, he was a strong, confident singer. Performing Ne-Yo's "So Sick" and Matchbox Twenty's "3 a.m.," he took second place in the "Stratford Idol" contest.

A few months later, Bieber was short on cash. His friends were going golfing, and he didn't have the money he needed to go along. So he came up with a plan. Stratford is home to the Stratford Shakespeare Festival, which stages a variety of plays and attracts many visitors each summer. Bieber took his guitar to one of the theaters where the festival is held. On the sidewalk outside, he opened his guitar case so that people passing by could toss money into it, and began to sing and play. Over the next few days, he earned enough money for the golfing trip—and a trip to Disneyland for himself and his mother. It was the first vacation they'd ever been able to afford.

YouTube Sensation

After "Stratford Idol," Bieber and his mother posted video clips of his performance on the YouTube web site. They wanted friends and relatives who hadn't been able to attend the show to be able to watch his performance. They also posted some new videos of him singing covers of songs by Chris Brown and Justin Timberlake. Before long, Bieber's postings were getting thousands of hits. Word was spreading, far beyond his family and friends, that Justin Bieber was a talent to be seen. It wasn't long before Mallette was contacted by people in the music business who wanted to sign Bieber to a contract. Without money to hire a lawyer, she didn't know how to sort out legitimate offers from those that would take advantage of her and her son. Not wanting to make a bad decision, she started trying to avoid the calls altogether.

That situation changed after Mallette was contacted by a talent agent named Scooter Braun. Best known for discovering rapper Asher Roth, Braun had worked as a marketing representative at So So Def Records before starting his own company. He had been looking for someone else's video on YouTube when he found Bieber's posting. Braun was very impressed. "I thought, 'I gotta find this kid.'" It took him a while to track down Mallette and get a message to her, and when he did, she only called him back "to get rid of him," according to Bieber. Instead, "they ended up having a two-hour conversation," he recalled. "My mom had that gut feeling. I think moms generally know when they have their gut feelings." Braun offered to fly Bieber and Mallette to Atlanta, Georgia, to meet with him, and they accepted. Braun won her trust and confidence, and she agreed to let him handle her son's music career.

11

Braun had some unusual ideas about the best way to get Bieber's career going. Many popular young music stars—including Britney Spears, Justin Timberlake, and Miley Cyrus—got their start in television programs on the Disney channel. Doing so allowed them to gain exposure and build confidence in their singing skills before trying to launch a full-blown music career. Braun felt that Bieber could, and should, take a different path. Without launching any sort of traditional publicity blitz, Braun began adding more videos to Bieber's YouTube channel. The videos didn't use backup musicians or expensive production elements; they were simply homemade videos showing off his voice, his musicianship, and his charm. Braun was counting on word of mouth to spread his young client's reputation. He thought fans would like to feel they had discovered Bieber on their own. He was right. Buzz about Bieber's videos spread quickly through the Internet, and his YouTube channel began to get millions of hits.

Wanted by Top Producers

Thanks to YouTube, Bieber had a large and growing fan base even before he had released a single. It wasn't just young girls who were talking about him, either. His reputation was growing in the music industry, but he still wasn't committed to any record company. Two influential producers emerged as the top competitors, trying to get him to sign with their labels: Justin Timberlake and Usher. Both of them had started out as teen singers and continued their success as adult artists and producers. Both of them saw huge potential in Bieber. "He had all the nuances of a classic artist," Usher recalled. "Very cute, for all the young girls, gotta have that. He had swagger. And most important, he had talent." Usher and Timberlake each felt that they could use their own experiences to help Bieber start a long-lasting career. The singer and his mother felt good about both producers, but in the end, Usher made a better offer. In October 2007, Bieber signed a contract with Usher's record label, Island Def Jam.

Even before signing Bieber, Usher saw his potential. "He had all the nuances of a classic artist," Usher recalled. "Very cute, for all the young girls, gotta have that. He had swagger. And most important, he had talent."

In spring 2008, Bieber and his mother left Stratford to move to Atlanta to focus on developing his career. The next months were busy. In addition to doing schoolwork with a tutor, Bieber spent time at voice lessons, working on original songs, and communicating with his fan base by way of Internet sites like Twitter, Facebook, MySpace, and, of course, YouTube. He also made guest appearances on television shows.

Knowing that the pressures on a rising teen star can be tough, Usher felt protective of his young protégé and spent plenty of time with him. "He's like a big brother to me," Bieber said of Usher. "We just hang out and don't really talk about music a lot. We go go-karting and to arcades and movies."

Bieber with Usher, his mentor, who signed him to the record label Island Def Jam.

My World

Bieber's first single, a love song titled "One Time," was released in spring 2009 and soon shot to the top of the *Billboard* Hot 100 chart. It was produced by Antonio "L.A." Reid, a Grammy Award-winning songwriter and producer who is also the chairman of Island Def Jam. The song's video featured a cameo appearance by Bieber's mentor, Usher. "Bieber's first *Billboard* Hot 100 single, 'One Time,' was an insanely catchy ode to young love that immediately won over fans. And so were his second, third, and fourth," wrote Monica Herrera, a music reviewer for *Billboard*. "It's hardly a stretch to imagine Bieber racking up more hits in the next decade to come."

Bieber's way of adding a dash of urban style and rhythm to sweet love songs was a winning combination, as shown in "One Time" and the songs that followed, "One Less Lonely Girl," "Favorite Girl," and "Love Me." With these songs, as reviewer Crystal Bell wrote in *Billboard*, "Bieber makes a strong case for why he's the next pop/R&B heartthrob." All of them shot to No. 1 on the charts, making him the first recording artist ever to have four No. 1 singles without having released an album. With each new single, his popularity increased still more. His promotional appearances around the U.S. and Canada began to attract thousands of wildly enthusiastic fans. In October 2009 Bieber appeared on "The Today Show" and drew a bigger crowd than any other musical artist that year, including Miley Cyrus.

My World was released in November 2009. With only seven tracks, it was really an extended-play (EP) recording, rather than a full-length album. In addition to the four hit singles that had already been released, it contained the tracks "Down to Earth," "Bigger," and "First Dance," which featured Usher. "Down to Earth" stood out from the romantic songs that made up the rest of the recording, with lyrics about painful relationships and a family breaking up. Despite its EP status, *My World* was included on the *Billboard* album charts, where it started out in the No. 6 spot. Within four months, over a million copies of *My World* had been sold.

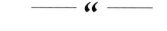

"He's like a big brother to me," Bieber said of Usher. "We just hang out and don't really talk about music a lot. We go go-karting and to arcades and movies."

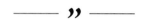

Biebermania

By that point, Bieber was already very popular with fans. But after the release of *My World,* the mobs of fans that greeted him at his appearances became even larger and more intense. The singer's road manager, Ryan Good, described it as "mass hysteria. Loud screaming, crying, passing out. It's amazing." On November 20, a scheduled appearance by Bieber at the Roosevelt Field Mall in Garden City, New York, turned into a near-riot. It was an afternoon event, but fans began arriving early in the morning. About 3,000 people eventually gathered. The crowd got out of control, and five people had to be sent to the hospital with minor injuries. By the time Bieber arrived, the police refused to let him enter the mall because the situation with the crowd was too dangerous. Similar mob scenes took place in Paris and in Australia. In both places, crowds were dispersed due to safety concerns.

Bieber appreciates his fans, and he enjoys performing. But the level of excitement from fans has been surprising to him. "I don't really understand it, because I've never had a musician I was that into," he said. "I just try to make it as fun for them as possible. For some of them, this might be the only time they'll get to meet me." He says that the crowds rushing at him can be a little scary. He now travels with bodyguards, who keep over-eager fans at a safe distance. He tries to maintain a personal connection with his fans by way of Twitter, Facebook, and other web sites, but at the same time, he's careful not to share too much detailed personal information. With over 162 million views of his videos on YouTube, 2.6 million fans on Facebook, and 1.7 million Twitter followers, privacy has become an issue.

Bieber with some of his fans at the Nickelodeon Kids' Choice Awards.

Singing for President Obama

Throughout late 2009 and early 2010, Bieber was busy performing. During one hectic weekend in December, he took part in a Christmas show at Madison Square Garden in New York City, flew to Las Vegas to tape a New Year's Eve television special, flew to Chicago for another performance, and ended up in Washington DC, where he was part of the annual "Christmas in Washington" concert. His fellow performers there included Mary J. Blige, Neil Diamond, Sugarland, Rob Thomas, and Usher. Bieber sang "Someday at Christmas," a song by Stevie Wonder. President Barack Obama and First Lady Michelle Obama were in the audience.

In February 2010, Bieber was part of "We are the World: 25 for Haiti," a recording made by a chorus of celebrity musicians to raise money for the victims of the earthquake that struck Haiti on January 12, 2010. The song was a remake of one written and produced 25 years earlier to raise money for famine relief in Africa. In March, Bieber performed at the Kids' Choice Awards in Los Angeles. He also celebrated his 16th birthday, receiving a Range Rover as a gift from Usher. In April, he performed for the Obamas again, this time at the White House Easter Egg Roll.

My World 2.0

On March 23, 2010, Bieber's album *My World 2.0* was released. It sold 283,000 copies that first day, putting it in the No. 1 spot on the *Billboard* album chart. He was the youngest solo male artist to have a No. 1 album since Stevie Wonder had done it at age 13, in 1963. Furthermore, Bieber's first album was still at No. 5. *My World 2.0* contained 10 tracks, and despite the album's title, the material was all new. Bieber got support from older artists such as Ludacris, who contributed to "Baby," the album's first hit single, and Sean Kingston, who took part in the playful "Eenie Meenie," about a girl who can't choose between two guys. On "Overboard," Bieber sang with Jessica Jarrell, an up-and-coming female vocalist.

Reviewing *My World 2.0* for the *Washington Post*, Chris Richards found it somewhat overproduced, but praised the young singer's abilities. "If we truly want the best of America's children, let us pause and give thanks for Justin Bieber," Richards wrote. "At its best, his voice is both powerful and adorable." More praise came from Jody Rosen, a reviewer for *Rolling Stone*. Rosen noted that while "Bieber's talent is not fully formed," those who dismiss *My World 2.0* because they think he is just another cute singer "are missing out on a seriously good pop record." Bieber supported the release of *My World 2.0* with still more high-profile appearances, including appearing as a musical guest on "Saturday Night Live." He also

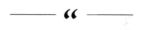

"I think that as my audience grows with me, that my lyrics will change and they'll be more directed for the older audience," Bieber commented. "I mean, right now I'm singing to young and old. I'm singing to basically anybody who wants to listen."

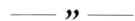

began preparing to launch his first full-blown tour late in June 2010. Talking about the fast-paced changes that have taken place in his life since he won the "Stratford Idol" competition, he said, "It has been overwhelming, but I love it."

Thinking ahead, Bieber hopes to attend college. He may major in English, because he likes writing. He has thought about getting into acting, and he wants to continue with his music, which he hopes will just keep getting better. "I think that as my audience grows with me, that my lyrics will change and they'll be more directed for the older audience," he commented. "I mean, right now I'm singing to young and old. I'm singing to basically anybody who wants to listen."

HOME AND FAMILY

Although they have a home base in Atlanta, Bieber and his mother are usually on the road, traveling in a group that includes his tutor, music

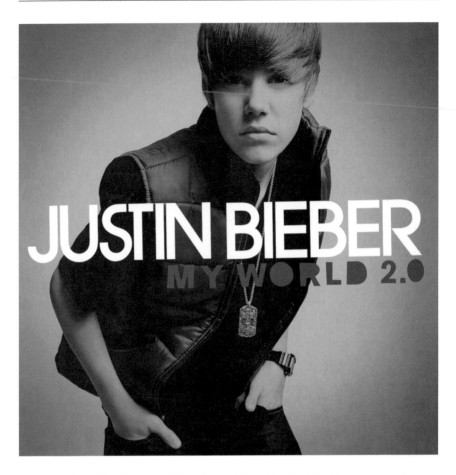

Bieber's first full album, My World 2.0, *debuted at the No. 1 spot on the charts.*

company representative, bodyguards, publicists, vocal coach, and road manager/stylist. "It's quite different coming where we're coming from to being driven around in limos," said Mallette. Despite his busy schedule, Bieber tries to make sure he has some time each week to do the things any kid his age would usually do, even if it means flying in a couple of his best friends from Stratford to hang out with him.

Bieber's mother is very important to him, and she travels everywhere with him. "She's been there since the beginning and has given up a lot for me, I'm very blessed to have her," he said. Mallette says she is proud of her son. "He's working really, really hard," she added. "But I'd probably be proud of him no matter what he did if he did his best and he was doing what he wanted to do and what God wanted him to do." Bieber also gives credit to his grandparents for helping to provide comfort and security for him and his mother in the days when she was a struggling single parent. "I definitely did not have a lot of money," Bieber recalled. "I couldn't afford to get a lot of new clothes a lot of times. But I had a roof over my head. I was very fortunate. I had my grandparents, I saw them a lot, they were very kind. So I grew up getting everything that I wanted."

FAVORITE MUSIC

Although Bieber likes all types of music, some of his favorite artists are Stevie Wonder, Michael Jackson, Boyz II Men, Ne-Yo, Drake, and Taylor Swift, about whom he said: "She tells stories that actually happened. Her songs are amazing."

HOBBIES AND OTHER INTERESTS

Bieber's favorite sports team is the Toronto Maple Leafs. He has played hockey with the Atlanta Knights, a AAA team. He enjoys soccer, go-karts, skateboarding, video games, and chess.

RECORDINGS

My World, 2009
My World 2.0, 2010

FURTHER READING

Periodicals

Billboard, Nov. 14, 2009, p.31; Mar. 27, 2010, p.18
Los Angeles Times, Apr. 10, 2010, p.D1
Maclean's, Dec. 28, 2009, p.16
New York Times, Dec. 14, 2009, p.C1; Jan. 3, 2010, p.1
People, Apr. 19, 2010, p.66
Rolling Stone, Jan. 21, 2010, p.22
Washington Post, Dec. 20, 2009, p.E1; Mar. 23, 2010, p.C1

Online Articles

http://www.msnbc.com
　　(MSNBC, "The Safe Sex Appeal of Justin Bieber," Apr. 21, 2010)
http://www.people.com
　　(People, "Five Things to Know about Justin Bieber," Jan. 8, 2010)
http://www.rollingstone.com/music/reviews
　　(Rolling Stone, "My World 2.0," Apr. 27, 2010)

ADDRESS

Justin Bieber
Island Records
825 Eighth Avenue
New York, NY 10019

WORLD WIDE WEB SITES

http://www.myspace.com/justinbieber
http://www.justinbiebermusic.com

Drew Brees 1979-

American Professional Football Quarterback with
the New Orleans Saints
Most Valuable Player of Super Bowl XLIV in 2010

BIRTH

Drew Christopher Brees was born on January 15, 1979, in Dallas, Texas. His parents, Chip Brees and Mina (Akins) Brees, were both lawyers. They named their first child after Drew Pearson, a star wide receiver for the Dallas Cowboys of the National Football League (NFL).

When Brees was seven years old, his family moved to Austin, Texas. Although his parents divorced a short time later, they maintained a friendly relationship. Drew and his younger brother, Reid, divided their time evenly between their parents' houses. Chip Brees later married Amy Hightower, and they had a daughter, Audrey, who is Drew's half-sister. Mina Brees later married Harley Clark, who originated the famous "hook 'em horns" hand gesture used by fans of the University of Texas Longhorns.

YOUTH

As a boy, Brees loved to play sports with his brother and neighborhood friends. "We played in the street, in the yard, using the garage as a backstop for pitching to each other," he recalled. "We were always going to the park. It was constant sports and activity."

> *As a boy, Brees loved to play sports with his brother and neighborhood friends. "We played in the street, in the yard, using the garage as a backstop for pitching to each other," he recalled. "We were always going to the park. It was constant sports and activity."*

Brees was an athletic kid who showed talent in a variety of sports. In baseball he played pitcher, shortstop, and third base. When he was 12 years old, he broke the Little League home run record for the city of Austin. He always wore jersey number 9 to be like his idol, Major League Baseball Hall of Famer Ted Williams.

Brees learned to play tennis from his mother, who had been a highly regarded player in her youth. "I wanted both Drew and his brother to be great tennis players, because that's my favorite sport," she admitted. "I was hoping he could be the next Pete Sampras or Andre Agassi." Brees ranked first in the state of Texas in the under-12 age group before he drifted away from the game. Still, the graceful footwork he developed as a tennis player has served him well in his football career.

Growing up, Brees's main exposure to football came from his maternal grandfather, Ray Akins. After fighting in the Pacific during World War II, Akins launched a career as a high-school football coach. The military discipline he instilled in his players helped make him a coaching legend in football-crazy Texas. Brees often visited his grandfather during the summer and attended his team's practice sessions. "He would tell us stories about the war and about football and about the value of hard work," he remembered. "He was an amazing man."

EDUCATION

Short and skinny as a kid, Brees did not play organized football until his freshman year at Westlake High School in Austin. Even then, he saw little action as the third-string quarterback on the junior varsity team. But Brees worked hard to learn the game and develop his skills. By the time he reached his junior year in 1995, he had earned the starting quarterback job on the varsity squad. Over the next two years, Brees led the Westlake Chaparrals to an amazing record of 28 wins, 0 losses, and 1 tie. Showing remarkable poise and accuracy as a passer, he threw for 5,416 yards and 50 touchdowns during those two seasons. Brees capped off his senior year in 1996 by leading his team to the Texas Class 5A state championship.

Despite his impressive performance on the football field, Brees attracted very little interest from college football recruiters when he graduated from high school in 1997. He was particularly disappointed not to receive scholarship offers from the two college football powerhouses in his home state, the University of Texas and Texas A&M University. "Believe me, we told them he was the most accurate passer we'd ever seen, that he was a great leader and a tough kid," remembered Westlake's offensive coordinator, Neal Lahue. "Nobody listened." Most college recruiters seemed concerned about his size. Brees was barely six feet tall, and recruiters worried that he would not be able to see over the opposing team's defensive line. "I just never believed that [height] mattered," he noted. "To play the quarterback position, it's all in the heart and the mind."

Purdue University Boilermakers

One of the few teams that offered Brees a full football scholarship was Purdue University in West Lafayette, Indiana. He jumped at the chance to play in the Big Ten Conference and to attend Purdue's prestigious Krannert School of Management. He spent his freshman year in 1997 learning Coach Joe Tiller's complex offensive system as the Boilermakers' backup quarterback.

As a sophomore in 1998, however, Brees won the starting job and showed phenomenal accuracy as a passer. He set Big Ten records in pass attempts (569), completions (361), completion percentage (63.4), passing yards (3,983), and touchdowns (39). "This guy has thrown the ball better than anybody we've had in this system," Tiller declared. Brees led the Boilermakers to an impressive 9-4 record for the season. He topped off his great year by throwing a last-second, game-winning touchdown pass in the Alamo Bowl to upset fourth-ranked Kansas State.

This outstanding 1998 season did not earn Brees much respect at the national level. Most football analysts gave credit for Purdue's success—and his

Brees's accuracy as a passer was evident early on, as in this 1999 Purdue game against Penn State.

impressive passing statistics—to Tiller's offensive system. "A lot of credit should go to the system," Brees acknowledged. "If you weren't throwing so many passes, you wouldn't be putting up all those numbers. But you still have to complete them. You have to know where to go with the football. The system does provide the opportunity, but you still have to execute."

Brees began to win over his doubters by turning in another strong performance during his junior season in 1999. He completed 337 of 554 passes (60.8 percent) for 3,909 yards and 25 touchdowns. He ranked third in the nation in total offense with 340.5 yards per game and finished fourth in the voting for the Heisman Trophy, awarded each year to the top player in college football. Brees also won the NCAA's first Socrates Award, presented annually to the nation's finest player in terms of academics, athletics, and community service. But his personal accolades did not translate into team success. Purdue finished the year with a 7-5 record and a loss to Georgia in the Outback Bowl.

Rather than leaving early for the NFL, Brees decided to return to Purdue for his senior year in 2000. His goal was to lead the Boilermakers to a Big Ten championship and earn a trip to the Rose Bowl for the first time since 1967. He had another outstanding year, completing 309 of 512 passes (60.4 percent) for 3,668 yards and 26 touchdowns. Purdue posted an 8-4 record to claim a share of the Big Ten title and a spot in the Rose Bowl.

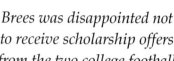

Brees was disappointed not to receive scholarship offers from the two college football powerhouses in his home state, the University of Texas and Texas A&M University. "Believe me, we told them he was the most accurate passer we'd ever seen, that he was a great leader and a tough kid," remembered Westlake's offensive coordinator, Neal Lahue. "Nobody listened."

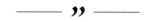

Although the Boilermakers lost to the Washington Huskies by a score of 34-24, Brees won the Maxwell Award as the nation's top collegiate player and finished third in the Heisman voting.

Brees graduated from Purdue in 2001 with a bachelor's degree in industrial management and manufacturing. His 3.4 grade point average earned him Academic All-American Player of the Year honors and an NFL post-graduate scholarship. He left Purdue as the Big Ten's all-time career leader in passing yards (11,792), total yards (12,693), touchdown passes (90), pass attempts (1,678), completions (1,026), and completion percentage (.611).

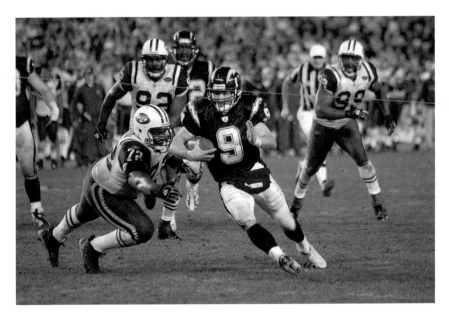

In 2005, Brees led the Chargers to the first round of the playoffs, where they lost to the New York Jets in overtime. Here, Brees runs for a first down at the one-yard line to set up the tying score.

CAREER HIGHLIGHTS

NFL—The San Diego Chargers

After completing his college football career, Brees was selected as the first pick in the second round of the 2001 NFL draft (32nd overall) by the San Diego Chargers. Although the Chargers had posted a dismal 1-15 record the previous year, fans hoped that the addition of Brees and running back LaDainian Tomlinson (San Diego's first-round pick) would revitalize the franchise. Brees signed a four-year contract with the Chargers worth $3.6 million, plus a $2 million signing bonus. He spent most of his rookie season watching from the bench as veteran quarterback Doug Flutie led the team to a 5-11 record.

Brees took over the starting job at the beginning of the 2002 season. He raised the expectations of Chargers fans early in the season by winning 6 of the first 7 games he started. San Diego came back to earth in the second half of the season, however, to finish the year at 8-8. The team continued to struggle at the outset of the 2003 season, losing 7 of the first 8 games. Brees threw 15 interceptions and only 11 touchdowns during this frustrating stretch. "I just felt helpless," he recalled. "I mean, it was hard on everyone, but I was very, very disappointed. Nothing ever felt right. We lost our first two games; then all of a sudden we were 0-5. Then people started pointing fingers, and the wheels just fell off the bus. I started pressing, trying to win each game on every play." Brees was benched for the final five games of the season in favor of Flutie, and the Chargers ended the year with a 4-12 record.

By the end of the disappointing 2003 season, San Diego management decided that the team needed to find a new quarterback. They used the first pick of the 2004 NFL draft to select quarterback Eli Manning, who quickly indicated that he had no desire to play for the Chargers. The team responded by trading Manning for another rookie quarterback, Philip Rivers. With Rivers on the roster, Brees found himself facing a major threat to his career. "People were turning their back on me and saying I couldn't play and I wasn't the right guy for this team," he acknowledged. "It was devastating. I was angry. No one wants to hear that he's not wanted. But once I got past it, I knew I could only worry about things in my control."

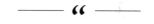

> *"People were turning their back on me and saying I couldn't play and I wasn't the right guy for this team,"* Brees acknowledged. *"It was devastating. I was angry. No one wants to hear that he's not wanted. But once I got past it, I knew I could only worry about things in my control."*

Making a Comeback

Prior to the start of the 2004 season, Brees analyzed every aspect of his game. He changed his training regimen and diet, and he redoubled his commitment to hard work and preparation. The changes paid off for both him and the Chargers. With Brees starting 15 games, San Diego went from worst to first in a single season and claimed the AFC West Division title with a 12-4 record. Brees led the way by passing for 3,159 yards, 27 touchdowns, and only 7 interceptions. His 104.8 passer rating ranked third in the NFL, and he earned his first Pro Bowl appearance. "I'm sure there was a lot of pressure on people that if I wasn't getting the job done, it was time to pull the plug and put the new guy in, you know, the future," he noted. "I don't play to prove people wrong. I don't want success so I can shove it in other people's faces. I play to win." Although the Chargers lost to the New York Jets in the first round of the playoffs, the league recognized Brees's remarkable career turnaround by naming him Comeback Player of the Year.

The successful 2004 campaign created a dilemma for San Diego management. They had signed Rivers to a six-year, $41 million contract, but now it appeared that Brees—who was eligible to become a free agent—gave the team its best chance to reach the playoffs again in 2005. They ultimately decided to designate Brees as the Chargers' "franchise player," which prevented him from becoming a free agent for one year in exchange for an $8 million contract. Brees responded by turning in another strong performance in 2005, throwing for 3,576 yards and 24 touchdowns with only 15 interceptions. It was not enough to lift the Chargers into the playoffs, however, as the team finished the season with a 9-7 record.

———— " ————

"When I visited New Orleans, I saw it all, the good and the bad," Brees recalled. "The city was devastated.... Cars lying on top of houses. Boats through living-room windows. I felt like I was driving through a World War II documentary. But I just thought, 'This is a chance to be part of something incredible—the rebuilding of an American city.' I felt like it was a calling. Like I was destined to be here."

———— " ————

Brees's departure from San Diego became a certainty in the final game of 2005 against the Denver Broncos. The quarterback dove to recover a fumble, and an opposing player landed on his throwing arm. Brees suffered a serious injury to his shoulder that required offseason surgery. "As much as I wanted the Chargers to resign me, I had a bad feeling that that might have been my last snap in a Chargers uniform," he related. "It was."

Joining the New Orleans Saints

The injury to Brees's throwing arm not only made the Chargers hesitant to resign him, but also limited his prospects on the free-agent market. One of the few teams that showed a consistent interest in acquiring his services was the New Orleans Saints. The Saints were beginning a rebuilding phase unlike any other in NFL history. On August 28, 2005, the city of New Orleans and other parts of the Gulf Coast had been devastated by Hurricane Katrina. This natural disaster took the lives of over 1,800 people and caused more than $80 billion in property damage. The Superdome, where the Saints played their home games, had served as an emergency shelter for 20,000 people during and immediately after the hurricane, and it sustained serious damage from wind and flooding. During the 2005 season, the Saints were forced to practice at a local high school, lift weights in

Brees joined the New Orleans Saints soon after Hurricane Katrina devastated the region. The Superdome, the team's home, was severly damaged by the disaster.

a tent, watch game films at a convention center, and play their home games in Baton Rouge, San Antonio, and even New Jersey. Partly as a result of all the disruptions, the Saints posted a dismal 3-13 record.

When Brees entered into negotiations with the Saints six months after Katrina, he and his wife came to New Orleans to survey the damage. "When I visited New Orleans, I saw it all, the good and the bad," he recalled. "The city was devastated. Brittany and I saw the Lower Ninth Ward. Unbelievable. Cars lying on top of houses. Boats through living-room windows. I felt like I was driving through a World War II documentary. But I just thought, 'This is a chance to be part of something incredible—the rebuilding of an American city.' I felt like it was a calling. Like I was destined to be here."

Brees signed a six-year, $60 million contract with the Saints. He became part of a major rebuilding process that included a new head coach, Sean Payton, and 27 new players. "The opportunity to come to a place that needs that rebuilding and resurgence, there's something to be said for being a part of that," Brees declared. "Obviously this city's trying to rebuild, trying to get back on track. We as a franchise are trying to rebuild, get back on track. The fact that we're going to be doing it together is a great thing."

Making the Playoffs

Everything came together to make 2006 a magical season for the Saints. With repairs completed at the Superdome, the team sold out every home game to season ticket holders—a first for any NFL team. The incredible fan support helped lift New Orleans to an 11-6 record and the second seed for the playoffs. Brees led the way with 356 completions for an NFL-leading 4,418 yards, with 26 touchdowns and only 11 interceptions. "We had a whole new offensive line, a rookie split end, other guys with little experience," Payton noted. "That's a lot of new pieces to the puzzle, and Drew has been the guy to bring them all together."

The Saints received a bye in the first round of the playoffs, then defeated the Philadelphia Eagles 27-24 to earn a spot in the NFC Championship game for the first time in franchise history. Although the Saints fell one game short of reaching the Super Bowl, losing to the Chicago Bears 39-16 in the NFC title game, New Orleans fans enjoyed the highly successful season. Brees was named to the 2006 NFL All-Pro Team in recognition of his contributions. "Really, the only team that believed in me was the Saints, and I feel like I owe them a big debt of gratitude," he said afterward. "I want to give them what they saw in me, which was a guy who could lead this team to a championship."

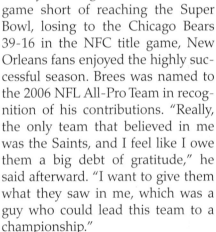

> "Really, the only team that believed in me was the Saints, and I feel like I owe them a big debt of gratitude," Brees stressed. "I want to give them what they saw in me, which was a guy who could lead this team to a championship."

Brees continued to put up great numbers in 2007. He finished the season with a league-leading 440 completions for 4,423 yards, with 28 touchdowns and 18 interceptions. The Saints struggled with injuries to several key players, however, and missed the playoffs with a 7-9 record. Brees had a remarkable year in 2008, when he became only the second quarterback in NFL history to pass for more than 5,000 yards in a season. His total of 5,069 yards narrowly missed beating the all-time record of 5,084 set by Dan Marino in 1984. Brees also led the league in completions with 413 and tied for first in touchdowns with 34. He was named Offensive Player of the Year and voted to his third career Pro Bowl appearance. Unfortunately, the Saints' defense struggled throughout the season and the team missed the playoffs with an 8-8 record. Still, Brees saw a great deal of potential for fu-

In 2007, the Saints made it to the NFC Championship game for the first time in franchise history. Brees is shown being sacked by Chicago Bears defender Israel Idonije (71) and Lance Briggs (55), and the Saints went on to lose 39-16.

ture success. "Three, four, five games all came down to one or two plays for us," he noted, "and if we make those plays, that's us in the Super Bowl."

The Saints Make It to the Super Bowl

Shortly before the start of the 2009 season, Brees received the sad news that his mother had passed away. But he did not allow his personal loss to distract him from his professional goal—marching the Saints all the way to the Super Bowl. The team got off to a fantastic start in the 2009 season, winning its first 13 games. The entire city of New Orleans rejoiced with each victory. Fans came up with a chant to express their belief that the Saints were unstoppable: "Who dat say they gonna beat them Saints?" The phrase "Who Dat" appeared on signs, T-shirts, and other merchandise all over town.

With Brees at the helm, Payton built the most potent offense in the NFL, averaging 40 points per game. "Drew and Sean have such a special relationship," said Brittany, Brees's wife. "They're so similar, such hard workers. They weren't the biggest or strongest. But they're smart guys who are going to figure out a way to win." Brees set a new NFL record by completing 70.62 percent of his passes (363 of 514), breaking a 27-year-old mark set by Ken Anderson. Adding 34 touchdowns and only 11 interceptions, Brees also earned a league-leading passer rating of 109.6.

After clinching a spot in the playoffs, New Orleans took the opportunity to rest some injured players and lost its final three games of the season. The Saints broke their losing streak as soon as the playoffs began, however, crushing the Arizona Cardinals 45-14 to win the division. The Saints moved on to the NFC Championship game, where they faced the Minnesota Vikings. The two teams waged an epic, seesaw battle through three quarters. With the game tied 28-28 and five minutes left to play, veteran quarterback Brett Favre drove the Vikings to the Saints' 33-yard line. Minnesota was then called for a penalty for having too many players on the field. The loss of yardage forced Favre to throw a pass, and Saints cornerback Tracy Porter picked it off for an interception. New Orleans kicked a field goal on its first possession of overtime to win 31-28 and reach the Super Bowl for the first time in franchise history.

Winning the Super Bowl and Earning the MVP Award

As Super Bowl XLIV approached, most analysts described the Saints as heavy underdogs. After all, Brees and his teammates had little playoff experience compared to their opponents, four-time league MVP Peyton Manning and the Indianapolis Colts. When the game got underway, the

In 2009, Brees led the league in passing, completing 70.62 percent of his passes and earning a rating of 109.6.

The Saint beat the Indianapolis Colts to win the 2010 Super Bowl 31-17, and Brees won the MVP award in recognition of his superlative play: 32 out of 39 passes completed for 288 yards and 2 touchdowns.

Colts jumped out to a 10-0 lead in the first quarter. The Saints overcame their early jitters, however, and scored two field goals in the second quarter to cut the deficit to 10-6 at halftime. Kicking off to start the second half, Payton shocked the Colts—as well as the millions of people watching the game—by trying an onside kick. The gamble worked perfectly, and the Saints drove straight down the field for a touchdown on the ensuing offensive possession to take a 13-10 lead. The Colts answered with a touchdown of their own, but the Saints added another field goal to close the gap to 17-16 at the end of the third quarter.

Still trailing by a point with 10 minutes left in regulation, Brees took matters into his own hands. He called his teammates into a huddle and told them, "Let's be special." Then he proceeded to hit seven passes to seven different receivers for a touchdown, followed by yet another pass to an eighth receiver for a 2-point conversion and a 24-17 lead. Porter, the Saints' defensive back who had made the key interception against Favre, sealed the victory by intercepting a Manning pass with three minutes remaining and running it back for a touchdown. The Saints won the Super Bowl by a score of 31-17.

Brees was an obvious choice for Most Valuable Player honors. He set a Super Bowl record by completing 82.1 percent of his passes (32 out of 39) for 288 yards and 2 touchdowns. "We played for so much more than ourselves—we played for our city. We played for the entire Gulf Coast region. We played for the entire 'Who Dat Nation,'" Brees said afterward. "Whoever thought that this could be happening? Eighty-five percent of the city was underwater. People were evacuating to places all over the country. Most people left not knowing whether New Orleans would ever come back, or if the organization would ever come back. But not only did the organization and the city come back. And so many of our core group of players came in that year as free agents, and we all looked at one another and said, 'We're going to rebuild together. We're going to lean on each other.' And that's what we've done."

In winning the Super Bowl MVP award, Brees proved that hard work, preparation, intelligence, and leadership ability can overcome limitations in physical size and strength. Since joining the Saints in 2006, he has passed for more yards (18,298) than any other NFL quarterback. He has raised the Saints franchise from the lowest point in its history all the way to the pinnacle of professional football. In the process, he has become a hero to the people of New Orleans and played a vital role in restoring the city's pride. "I get people stopping me on the street every day, like 20 times a day, telling me how great it makes them feel and how it just helps them go about their day and rebuild their life," Brees stated. "It means a tremendous amount."

MARRIAGE AND FAMILY

Brees married Brittany Dudchenko, whom he met while they were both students at Purdue. They have a son, Baylen Robert Brees, who was born on his father's 30th birthday in 2009, and they are expecting another child in late 2010.

HOBBIES AND OTHER INTERESTS

Other than spending time with his family, Brees's main hobby is collecting military coins. He is also known as one of the most active NFL players in terms of volunteer work and community service. Since founding the Brees Dream Foundation in 2003, he and his wife have raised or committed over $4.5 million for various causes. The foundation has helped rebuild schools, parks, playgrounds, and athletic fields in New Orleans. It gives away 300 bicycles to needy children every year at Christmas. It also provides care for

———— " ————

By leading the Saints to a Super Bowl championship, Brees became a hero to the people of New Orleans and played a vital role in restoring the city's pride. "I get people stopping me on the street every day, like 20 times a day, telling me how great it makes them feel and how it just helps them go about their day and rebuild their life," he stated. "It means a tremendous amount."

———— " ————

cancer patients and funding to advance cancer research.

The foundation sponsors a number of annual charity events, including an NFL players golf tournament, a youth football gridiron challenge, and Habitat for Humanity home-building projects. One of Brees's favorite events is the Brees on the Seas deep-sea fishing excursion, in which he takes seriously ill children and their families out on a boat in the Gulf of Mexico. "When you see the look on these kids' faces when they catch a fish—some of them have never caught a fish in their life—sometimes that's the best therapy, as good as any medicine you could give them," he related.

Finally, Brees serves as a spokesman for the NFL Play 60 program, which encourages American kids to engage in physical activity for at least 60 minutes per day to prevent obesity and achieve better health. Brees has received several honors for his community service, including the 2006 Walter Payton Man of the Year Award from the NFL and the 2008 Horizon Award from the U.S. Congress.

WRITINGS

Coming Back Stronger; Unleashing the Power of Adversity, 2010 (with Chris Fabry)

HONORS AND AWARDS

Texas High School 5A Offensive Player of the Year: 1996
Big Ten Conference Player of the Year: 1998, 2000
Socrates Award: 1999
Maxwell Award: 2000
Academic All-American Player of the Year: 2000
NFL Comeback Player of the Year: 2004
NFL Pro Bowl: 2004, 2006, 2008, 2009

NFC Offensive Player of the Year: 2006, 2008, 2009

NFL Walter Payton Man of the Year: 2006

Horizon Award for Making a Difference in the Lives of Youth (U.S. Congress): 2008

NFL Offensive Player of the Year: 2008

Super Bowl XLIV Most Valuable Player: 2010

ESPY Awards (ESPN): 2010 (four awards, Best Male Athlete, Best Championship Performance, Best NFL Player, and Best Team (with the New Orleans Saints)

FURTHER READING

Books

Brees, Drew, and Chris Fabry. *Coming Back Stronger: Unleashing the Power of Adversity,* 2010

DiPrimio, Pete. *Drew Brees,* 2010 (juvenile)

Donnes, Alan, and Chris Myers. *Patron Saints: How the Saints Gave New Orleans a Reason to Believe,* 2007

Savage, Jeff. *Amazing Athletes: Drew Brees,* 2010 (juvenile)

Periodicals

Austin Business Journal, Nov. 30, 2001, p.23

Los Angeles Times, Feb. 8, 2010, p.C1

San Diego Union Tribune, Jan. 21, 2007

Sporting News, Aug. 21, 2000, p.78; Nov. 6, 2000, p.58; Aug. 17, 2009, p.55

Sports Illustrated, Aug. 16, 1999, p.56; Apr. 30, 2001, p.56; Nov. 15, 2004, p.61; Sep. 21, 2009, p.52; Jan. 18, 2010, p.54; Feb. 15, 2010, p.30

Sports Illustrated Kids, Winter 2008, p.21; Dec. 2009, p.24

Texas Monthly, Jan. 2002, p.82

USA Today, Nov. 17, 2004, p.C1; Sep. 8, 2006, p.F14; Oct. 2, 2009, p.C1; Oct. 26, 2009, p.C5; Feb. 8, 2010, p.C8

ADDRESS

Drew Brees

New Orleans Saints

5800 Airline Drive

Metairie, LA 70003

WORLD WIDE WEB SITES

http://www.drewbrees.com

http://www.neworleanssaints.com

Ursula M. Burns 1958-

American Business Executive
CEO of Xerox
First African-American Woman to Head a Fortune
500 Company

BIRTH

Ursula M. Burns was born on September 20, 1958, the second
of her mother's three children. Her father played little role in
her life, and it was her mother, Olga, who supported the family by running a home-based daycare business, taking in iron-
ing, and cleaning offices.

YOUTH

Burns grew up in New York City, living with her mother, brother, and sister in a low-income housing project on Delancey Street on the Lower East Side of Manhattan. "The gangs were there, and the drug addicts were there," she recalled in the *New York Times*. "There were lots of Jewish immigrants, fewer Hispanics and African Americans, but the common denominator and great equalizer was poverty."

> "I came from a very poor single-parent household," Burns explained, "but from a woman who was extremely confident, very amazing, and had nothing but outstanding expectations of me and my siblings. So while business wasn't the goal, success was the goal.... My mother was the person who instilled in me that it is possible to just go after it."

Despite the difficult circumstances, Burns's mother dedicated herself to providing for her children and insisted that they take responsibility for their lives. Her example and guidance were a great influence on her daughter. "I came from a very poor single-parent household," Burns explained, "but from a woman who was extremely confident, very amazing, and had nothing but outstanding expectations of me and my siblings. So while business wasn't the goal, success was the goal.... My mother was the person who instilled in me that it is possible to just go after it." Decades later, after she became a high-ranking executive, she paid tribute to her mother by placing a motto on her office wall: "Don't do anything that wouldn't make your Mom proud."

EDUCATION

Another important factor in Burns's childhood was her schooling, and in this area, too, her mother played a decisive role. Even though the family had very little money, Olga Burns found a way to send all of her children to private Catholic schools because she believed that doing so would keep them safe and provide them a quality education. Ursula Burns spent the final years of her secondary schooling at Cathedral High School in New York City and earned her diploma in 1976.

Throughout her school years, math was a favorite subject for Burns, and she decided to pursue college studies in engineering. Accepted into a number of universities, including several prestigious Ivy League schools, she opted to attend Polytechnic Institute of New York University. She was able to afford her college tuition because of assistance she received from the New York State Higher Education Opportunity Program, which provides scholarship funds and other help to deserving students from disadvantaged backgrounds. She graduated in 1980 with a Bachelor of Science (BS) degree. She then enrolled in a graduate program in mechanical engineering at Columbia University and earned a Master of Science (MS) degree in mechanical engineering the following year.

CAREER HIGHLIGHTS

In the summer of 1980, right after she completed her undergraduate degree, Burns began an internship at the Xerox Corporation, a large U.S. company that had helped pioneer the development of photocopying technology and went on to become a leading manufacturer of document production equipment. Impressed with her abilities, Xerox helped pay for her graduate studies at Columbia and gave her a position as a contract worker and then as a full-time employee after she earned her master's degree.

Burns began working as an engineer in the areas of product planning and development. "From the day I walked in, I was trained by Xerox to believe that what I did was real and had real impact," she recalled. "It was, 'Here's a problem; can you solve it?' … So therefore I got confident." She advanced through a number of different positions during the early 1980s, and in 1987 she moved into management, overseeing engineering teams working on Xerox products. At that point, she was still less than 30 years old, and she often encountered individuals who were surprised that a woman of her age was supervising important projects. "People would ask, 'So where is the boss?'" Burns later recalled. "I'd say, 'I am.' And they'd ask, 'How old are you?'"

Race, Gender, and Performance

While her age attracted a certain amount of attention, Burns was also unique for another reason: she was a high-ranking black female in a profession where there were relatively few minorities and even fewer females of color. Throughout her career, she was something of a pioneer in this regard, and her presence was a sign of change. Since the 1960s, Xerox had been making a focused effort to create greater racial and gender diversity among its employees, one of many businesses to undertake that step. As Burns rose through the ranks, she was often viewed as a symbol of the progress that Xerox had made in that regard.

While the corporation's diversity policy brought a wider array of people into important positions in the workforce, it also created controversy.

Burns with a colleague at Xerox.

When minorities and women were hired and promoted, questions were sometimes raised about whether they were truly qualified for their new positions or whether they were simply being advanced in order to meet the company's goal of becoming more inclusive.

Burns has faced this issue throughout her career. While she agreed that Xerox's policies aided her progress, she has argued that the main factors behind her success are her abilities and her accomplishments. "I'm in this job because I believe I earned it through hard work and high performance," she explained. "Did I get some opportunities early in my career because of my race and gender? Probably.... I imagine race and gender got the hiring guys' attention. And then the rest was really up to me." In another interview, she explained her views in a different way. "Being a black woman is who I am and I can't control that. But being the youngest person to pass through all the gates is what I did have control over.... The fact that I did it faster than others has nothing to do with race and gender. It was my performance."

Telling It Like It Is

In addition to her skills as an engineer and manager, Burns developed a reputation for being a "straight shooter" who was not afraid to speak her mind. It was that quality that led to the next phase of her career at the company. In 1989, she attended a meeting where Wayland Hicks, the vice president of marketing and customer operations at Xerox, responded to a question about the company's diversity initiatives. Feeling that Hicks did not defend the program forcefully enough, she debated the senior executive openly at the meeting. Soon after, Hicks summoned her to his office. Burns feared that she might be fired, but instead, the vice president asked if she would be interested in meeting with him on a regular basis to discuss issues at the company. "She was enormously curious," Hicks explained. "She wanted to know why we were doing some things at the time, and she was always prepared in a way that I thought was very refreshing."

In early 1990, Burns became executive assistant to Hicks. In that role, she attended high level meetings, traveled on business trips, and helped her boss to get things accomplished. She also received a crash course in senior management, with Hicks passing on his knowledge about leadership. The job brought her in frequent contact with other executives at Xerox, and she got the opportunity to share her opinions with them as well. Paul Allaire, the person who then headed Xerox as chief executive officer (CEO), was impressed with her candor and ideas, and in 1991, he asked her to become his executive assistant. In that position, Burns spent even more time away from home, devoting 40 percent of her work hours to corporate trips in which she and the CEO courted new clients and kept tabs on Xerox's far-flung global operations.

For Burns, the main factors behind her success are her abilities and her accomplishments. "I'm in this job because I believe I earned it through hard work and high performance," she explained. "Did I get some opportunities early in my career because of my race and gender? Probably.... I imagine race and gender got the hiring guys' attention. And then the rest was really up to me."

The next assignment for Burns was to oversee various business units within the company. Her success in that role led to a promotion to vice president and general manager of the Workgroup Copier Business in 1995, which required her to relocate to London, England. After two years there, she returned to the United States to head the Departmental Copier Business Unit. In 1999, she took another step toward the top when she was named vice president of Worldwide Business Services.

Troubled Times at Xerox

While Burns's personal career was thriving, Xerox was not faring so well. By the late 1990s, the company was teetering on the edge of bankruptcy due to changing market conditions and several major missteps. Faced with tough competition from other copier companies, it lagged behind its rivals in developing cutting-edge products and technology. A new CEO replaced Allaire in 1999 and shook things up by cutting 14,000 jobs and reorganizing the sales force, but the changes did little to improve business. Profits fell sharply, and in 2000, the U.S. Securities and Exchange Commission began investigating accounting problems at Xerox. The value of the company's stock plummeted as shareholders lost faith in its direction.

"Being a black woman is who I am and I can't control that," Burns pointed out. "But being the youngest person to pass through all the gates is what I did have control over.... The fact that I did it faster than others has nothing to do with race and gender. It was my performance."

Burns began to have her own doubts about her employer during this period and decided to leave. "It was not because of more money," she said. "It was just, 'What's going on here? What is this place?'" Once she informed her superiors of her decision, however, they pleaded with her to stay and help the ailing company. Surprised that they valued her so much, she ultimately decided to remain with Xerox, and she began to realize that she might have a chance of rising to the very top of the corporation. Around this time, she was handed new responsibilities, becoming senior vice president of Corporate Strategic Services in 2000.

Meanwhile, Xerox looked to a new CEO, company veteran Anne M. Mulcahy, to change its fortunes. Shortly after taking the helm in August 2001, Mulcahy began putting together a "turnaround team" to guide the corporation out of trouble, and she asked Burns to join the group. The two women quickly formed a very productive partnership. As the senior executive, Mulcahy focused on the corporation's finances and on convincing people inside and outside the company that Xerox could turn the corner.

Burns with Anne M. Mulcahy, whom she succeeded as CEO.

For her part, Burns was given responsibility for managing many of the details of how the business was run. "Anne had so many other things to focus on," Burns later explained. "The employee base was nervous, our customers were really unhappy, our investors were panicking. While she was focusing on other things, she just gave me a mandate to fix this thing."

Managing a Crisis

Burns's assignment was especially challenging because she had to make the company smaller and more efficient. Xerox was too far in debt and spending too much money, and Mulcahy asked Burns to find a way to cut $2 billion in costs. To accomplish that goal, she had to make many tough decisions that had a profound effect on the company. She masterminded a plan to hire other businesses to handle much of Xerox's manufacturing, and she greatly reduced the number of managers in the corporation. Moreover, Burns negotiated new contracts with unionized employees that helped save additional money. In the end, the Xerox workforce was reduced by nearly 40 percent.

While drastically cutting costs, Mulcahy and Burns also needed to improve the products offered by Xerox. Towards that end, a new line of copiers and printers was introduced, including innovative color models. In time, the changes put in place by the two executives began to pay off. By 2007, the company's debt was half of what it had been five years before, net earnings had greatly increased, and its stock price was on the rebound. The fear of bankruptcy that had previously hung over Xerox had been banished.

> "This old notion that work is drudgery is nonsense," Burns asserted at a commencement ceremony, and she encouraged the young graduates to find a similar sense of excitement and dedication in their own careers. "Most days—even back when Xerox was under siege—I could not wait to get to the office," she recalled. "I love my work—and you should too."

While the company's turnaround was a collaborative effort, Burns has claimed credit for much of the restructuring that took place, noting that "Ten percent of that was Anne [Mulcahy], 90 percent was me." Mulcahy agrees that Burns was instrumental in the changes that took place and has explained that "Ursula absorbs problems like a sponge. Once she takes them on, it's 'Let's go!'" Burns has been equally appreciative of Mulcahy and has viewed her as a role model, not only for her business achievements but for her ability to pursue a high level career while raising a family.

Reaching the Top

Burns acquired a series of new job titles while helping Xerox return to health. In 2001, she became president of Document Systems and Solutions, and the following year, she was named senior vice president of Business Group Operations, which provides more than 80 percent of the company's sales. With her success in helping guide the Xerox turnaround, there was a great deal of speculation that Burns was destined to one day become CEO.

*Burns is shown accepting the National Medal of Technology
of behalf of Xerox from President George W. Bush.*

As with most large corporations, Xerox employs a senior leadership system
in which an individual who is expected to become CEO first takes the position of president, which is the second-highest office in the business. In
April 2007, Burns officially received that title and was also made a member
of the board of directors—the group that governs the company and repre-
sents its stockholders.

It was Mulcahy who had chosen Burns as her successor, but the two women
found that the leadership transition was not entirely smooth, despite their
close relationship. They engaged in several weeks of intense discussions to

As CEO of Xerox, Burns has taken a prominent role,
which often includes public speaking.

decide how they would divide their responsibilities during the period before Burns finally became CEO. But, as in their previous collaborations, the two reached a successful compromise. "I definitely want to lead this company," Burns said in *Fortune*. "But I do not want to lead it until Anne doesn't want to." Over the next two years, Burns got further guidance about the CEO's responsibilities and learned that there were many fine points to leading the company. Mulcahy provided her with valuable advice, which included tips on how to motivate employees and suggestions about keeping a "poker face" so that others would not be able to easily read Burns's emotions.

Finally, on July 1, 2009, the preparation came to an end, and Ursula Burns took over as the chief executive officer of the Xerox Corporation. In addition to being a major achievement for Burns herself, it was a significant milestone in American business history. She was the first African-American woman to become the CEO of a Fortune 500 company, and when Mulcahy turned the leadership over to Burns, it was the first time that a woman succeeded another woman in heading a corporation of that size.

Looking to the Future

Once she took her place in the CEO's office, or "C-suite," Burns quickly showed that she was willing to take the company in a new direction. In

September 2009, less than two months after she took charge, Xerox announced that it was buying another business, Affiliated Computer Services. The move is intended to strengthen the corporation's ability to provide a full range of document services. Rather than simply selling and servicing equipment, as it has in the past, Xerox plans to help customers with tasks such as payroll, accounting, and other information-related functions. Burns has identified this as an important new area that will be a major focus in the years ahead.

Another important element that Burns has stressed since taking charge of the company is the need for employees to talk honestly with one another about important issues in the workplace. This emphasis is not surprising given her own history of speaking her mind. "I want us to stay civil and kind, but we have to be frank," she said, "and the reason we can be frank is because we are all in the same family."

In directing her corporate "family," Burns plans to lead by example, which means showing her employees that she has is extremely involved in the company and working as hard as they are to attain success. This is the same approach that she has followed since moving into management, and she believes it is much more important than trying to appear calm and assured at all times, as many senior executives strive to do. "One of the things I was told early on is that you should never let them see you sweat," she noted. "I remember hearing that and saying: 'Oh my God! I think that they have to see you sweat.'"

Though her job comes with many challenges, Burns remains passionate about what she does. "This old notion that work is drudgery is nonsense," she asserted in a 2009 commencement address, and she encouraged the young graduates to find a similar sense of excitement and dedication in their own careers. "Most days—even back when Xerox was under siege—I could not wait to get to the office," she recalled. "I love my work—and you should too."

MARRIAGE AND FAMILY

Burns lives in Rochester, New York, with her husband, Lloyd F. Bean. She and Bean, a former scientist at Xerox, were married in 1988. She has two children, a stepson named Malcolm and a daughter named Melissa. Though her total yearly compensation for 2009 was estimated to be more than $11 million, she refuses to adopt all the trappings of an affluent lifestyle. She still does her own shopping and drives her own car rather than using chauffeured vehicles.

As is common with high level executives, Burns devotes a lot of hours to her work and has had to be creative in finding ways to meet both her professional and personal responsibilities. At certain points in her career, she was away from home for extended periods. Back in 1992, for instance, she noted that "I see my husband two, maybe three times a month. We've been married for three years, but we've only had the same home base for one year. He lives in our official home in Rochester, and I live in a townhouse in Stamford [Connecticut]."

> "
>
> *"I meet a lot of women today who actually say they are not going to have a family because they want to be executives.*
>
> *My response is what do the two have to do with each other? You can do all those things ... if you aren't trying to balance them perfectly."*
>
> "

To deal with the great demands, of her job, Burns tries to remain flexible and allows herself to take time away from work when necessary. "If you do call in [to the office] or just don't show up occasionally, nobody will die," she said. "People will actually applaud that you made a reasonable choice." Overall, she feels that having children need not be a hindrance to a successful career as long as female employees remain realistic about what can be accomplished. "I meet a lot of women today who actually say they are not going to have a family because they want to be executives. My response is what do the two have to do with each other? You can do all those things ... if you aren't trying to balance them perfectly."

HOBBIES AND OTHER INTERESTS

Burns assists a number of charitable and educational organizations, serving on the boards of the National Center on Addiction and Substance Abuse at Columbia University, the National Academy Foundation, the Massachusetts Institute of Technology, and the University of Rochester. Encouraging young people to become interested in technology is one of her major priorities. She is a board member for FIRST (Foundation for the Inspiration and Recognition of Science and Technology). Moreover, in November 2009 President Barack Obama named her as one of the people to lead the "Educate to Innovate" campaign that is intended to improve students' skills in science, technology, engineering, and math (STEM).

Because of the expertise that she has gained in her many years as a senior manager, Burns has also been invited to help guide other companies and organizations. She is a member of the boards of directors for American Express Corporation, Boston Scientific Corporation, and the National Association of Manufacturers.

HONORS AND AWARDS

50 Most Powerful Black Executives in America (*Fortune*): 2002

Annual List of Global Business Influentials (*Time*/CNN): 2003

50 Most Important Blacks in Technology (*U.S. Black Engineer and Information Technology*): 2003-05

75 Most Powerful African Americans in Corporate America (*Black Enterprise*): 2005

50 Most Powerful Black Women in Business (*Black Enterprise*): 2006

50 Most Powerful Women in American Business (*Fortune*): 2006

Inductee, Denice Dee Denton Women Engineers Hall of Fame (Maseeh College of Engineering and Computer Science, Portland State University): 2009

National Equal Justice Award (NAACP Legal Defense and Educational Fund): 2009

75 Most Powerful Women in Business (*Black Enterprise*): 2010

FURTHER READING

Periodicals

Black Enterprise, Feb. 1992, p.246; Feb. 2010, p.88

BusinessWeek, June 8, 2009, p.18

Current Biography Yearbook, 2007

Fortune, Oct. 15, 2007, p.78

International Herald Tribune, May 2, 2007, p.14

New York Times, June 1, 2003; May 22, 2009; Sep. 29, 2009; Feb. 21, 2010

Online Articles

http://people.forbes.com/profile/ursula-m-burns/4692
    (Forbes, "Ursula M. Burns," no date)

http://topics.nytimes.com
    (New York Times, "Ursula M. Burns," multiple articles, various dates)

http://www.nytimes.com/2010/02/21/business/21xerox.html
    (New York Times, "Xerox's New Chief Tries to Redefine Its Culture," Feb. 20, 2010)

http://topics.wsj.com/person/index
(Wall Street Journal, "Ursula M. Burns," no date)

ADDRESS

Ursula M. Burns
Xerox Headquarters
45 Glover Avenue
PO Box 4505
Norwalk, CT 06856-4505

WORLD WIDE WEB SITE

http://news.xerox.com/pr/xerox/ursula-m-burns.aspx

Gustavo Dudamel 1981-

Venezuelan Classical Music Conductor
Music Director of the Los Angeles Philharmonic

BIRTH

Gustavo Adolfo Dudamel Ramirez was born on January 26, 1981, in Barquisimeto, the capital city of Lara, Venezuela. He comes from a musical family—his father, Oscar, played trombone in a salsa band for a living and worked with the local orchestra from time to time, while his mother taught voice lessons at a nearby conservatory. Due to his parents' occupations and the rich tradition of popular music in his hometown, he attended numerous live performances before he could even speak.

YOUTH

Dudamel's parents lived with his grandparents while he was a child, and his grandmother, Engracia de Dudamel, introduced him to classical music at an early age. She remembers taking Dudamel to see his father perform in a classical concert in Barquisimeto. "He was very small, I thought he was going to fall asleep," she recounted to the *New York Times*. "And he was completely attentive to details of the instruments. He said, 'Grandmother, I like this music.'"

Inspired to take up an instrument, Dudamel tried to play the trombone like his father, but discovered that his arms were too short. Instead, he entertained himself by setting up an imaginary orchestra of Lego figures. "I identified with the conductor a lot," he explained. "I thought, how interesting that the conductor uses an instrument that no one hears. I fell in love with it. I began to conduct in my house, arranging dolls as the orchestra. I'd put on a record and conduct, like theater." He wasted no time becoming familiar with the classics. "The first score that I had in my hand was Beethoven's Fifth, when I was seven years old," he remembered. "The first piece I played with an orchestra was Beethoven's Fifth."

> "I identified with the conductor a lot," Dudamel explained. "I thought, how interesting that the conductor uses an instrument that no one hears. I fell in love with it. I began to conduct in my house, arranging dolls as the orchestra. I'd put on a record and conduct, like theater."

Dudamel's strong reaction to this particular piece of music is something that he shares with his fellow countrymen. "In Venezuela we have a special connection with Beethoven. For us Beethoven is a symbol," he explained. "In Beethoven, you have more than music. It teaches you not only about music but about life, real life. The Fifth of Beethoven is a man searching for his destiny, and trying to live with his destiny. And for a kid who lives in our society today, it's a great thing to learn. Because a big percentage of the musicians come from very poor backgrounds, they've had a tough life. And to have the chance to get in touch with this symphony means not only to play music but also to give a very special meaning to that music." Moreover, Dudamel has acknowledged his supportive family for providing him with a strong personal foundation. "[It's] about values, and I think my values are really, really [down to] earth," he claimed. "My fami-

Dudamel developed a passion for conducting at a young age.

ly was giving me values, and the [educational] system of Venezuela was giving me values, to know what I am."

EDUCATION

At age four, Dudamel began taking violin lessons through El Sistema, a music education system designed to help Valenzuela's poor children. El Sistema was founded in 1975 by José Antonio Abreu, a Venezuelan economist who wanted to nurture his country's young musicians. Noting that many of the players in Venezuela's orchestras were foreigners, Abreu convinced the government to fund his program, which exists to this day. In fact, El Sistema has been so successful that it has inspired similar programs in other countries and has served as the focus of a documentary entitled *El Sistema: Music to Change Life*, which features Dudamel conducting the Simón Bolívar Youth Orchestra of Venezuela (SBYOV).

El Sistema trains children to play an instrument and then places them in a youth orchestra. Not only does this provide an educational structure for musically oriented kids, but it also presents a positive alternative to a criminal lifestyle. "[Many] boys from my school got pulled into gangs and drugs," Dudamel explained. "But those who came along to the sistema were saved. In a youth orchestra you must be in harmony with those around you. This makes you a good person, I think." According to Abreu,

Dudamel is an excellent example of El Sistema's importance and success. "Gustavo is the highest and most sublime expression of what [El Sistema] is," Abreu told the *Los Angeles Times*. "His musical and intellectual condition were acquired within the bosom of [El Sistema] and within the country." Now that Dudamel has risen to international fame, he has expressed great pride in his roots and is a champion of the music program that nurtured his talent. "I am a product of the sistema, and in the future, I will be here, working for the next generations," he affirmed.

During his training in El Sistema, Dudamel studied violin under José Luis Jiménez at the Jacinto Lara Conservatory at age 10. When he was 13, Jiménez allowed him to conduct a program that consisted of renaissance dances and Wolfgang Amadeus Mozart's "Ein kleine Nachtmusik." He then studied at the Latin American Academy of Violin under noted maestro José Francisco del Castillo. Proving himself a musical prodigy, he began taking lessons to become a conductor at age 15 and was named director of the state youth orchestra that same year. One of his instructors, conductor Rodolfo Saglimbeni, was instantly impressed by the young student. "When [Dudamel] was leading the state youth orchestra," Saglimbeni recalled in the *Los Angeles Times*, "maestro Abreu asked me to go there and give him some advice and I immediately knew I was in front of a special person with extraordinary capacities for music."

> *At an early age, Dudamel learned the importance of the relationship between a conductor and his players. "I can be very firm," he explained, "but I also believe that the conductor is just another musician in the orchestra. When you are clear about this, it creates a magical atmosphere where everyone feels they can contribute."*

At an early age, Dudamel learned the importance of the relationship between a conductor and his players. "I can be very firm," he explained, "but I also believe that the conductor is just another musician in the orchestra. When you are clear about this, it creates a magical atmosphere where everyone feels they can contribute." As he continued to perform with many of the same musicians throughout his teenage years, he discovered that this bond grows stronger over time. "The relationship between the orchestra and me is so easy that sometimes in rehearsal I don't have to tell them anything—they are waiting for my hands and my movements," he commented.

CAREER HIGHLIGHTS

At the age of 18, Dudamel was appointed music director of the Simón Bolívar Youth Orchestra of Venezuela (SBYOV). Based in the Venezuelan capital of Caracas, the SBYOV was designed to place the most advanced students from El Sistema into a working environment that emphasizes the importance of the group while fostering the talents of the individual. Holding this position allowed him to hone his skills as a community leader of sorts. "In Venezuela, the most important thing is the orchestra," he stated. "You create a community, with a shared objective. That's why [the SBYOV] has such a special sound: we have learned together, as a collective."

In 2000, Dudamel performed throughout Germany with the SBYOV. This tour included a critically acclaimed performance at the prestigious Berlin Philharmonie. Later that year he was appointed as music director of the Youth Orchestra of the Andean Countries and was selected as principal conductor of the Youth Orchestra of the Americas. Incredibly, he achieved all of this before he turned 20.

"The relationship between the orchestra and me is so easy that sometimes in rehearsal I don't have to tell them anything—they are waiting for my hands and my movements," Dudamel commented.

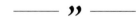

Breaking onto the World Stage

Dudamel gained more exposure in 2002 when he was chosen to perform during the UNICEF Children's Summit in New York City. That same year he won a Conductor's Academy competition that granted him a weeklong master class with renowned conductors Kurt Masur and Christoph von Dohnanyi. In 2004 he traveled to Bamberg, Germany, to compete in the Gustav Mahler International Conducting Competition. Not only did this mark his first performance with a professional orchestra, but he also won the competition. One of the judges for the Mahler Prize was Finnish composer Esa-Pekka Salonen, who was the music director of the Los Angeles Philharmonic at the time. Salonen was so impressed by Dudamel's performance that he invited him to conduct the Los Angeles Philharmonic at the Hollywood Bowl.

The concert was a huge success, prompting Mark Swed of the *Los Angeles Times* to proclaim that Dudamel "accomplished something increasingly rare and difficult at the Hollywood Bowl. He got a normally restive audience's full, immediate, and rapt attention. And he kept it." His reputation began to

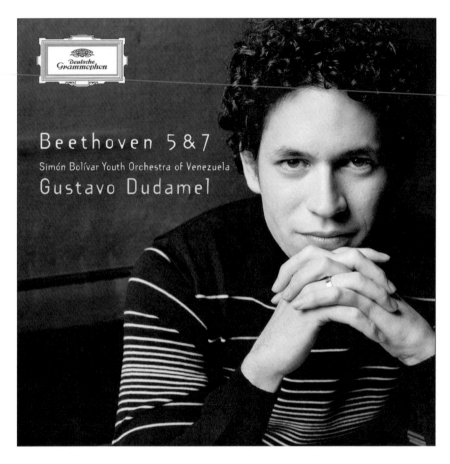

*Dudamel has always felt a special connection with Beethoven's music,
which he selected for his first recording.*

spread, with critics comparing him to Simon Rattle, the highly esteemed
British conductor who rose to prominence at a very young age during the
1970s. In fact, Rattle himself told London's *Daily Telegraph* that Dudamel
was "the most astonishingly gifted conductor I've ever come across."

When asked whether older musicians ever felt resentful about being led by
a person half their age, Dudamel acknowledged that "Of course, it sometimes happens. But for me the most important thing is to keep their respect, and from those people I always feel like I have something to learn. I
always try to share something with all the musicians, but especially with
those musicians that maybe gave me some resistance, I always try to get
closer to them."

Signing a Record Deal and Performing Abroad

In 2005 Dudamel was offered a recording contract by Deutsche Grammophon, one of the leading classical music recording labels. For his debut he recorded *Ludwig van Beethoven: Symphonies nos. 5 & 7*, an SBYOV performance of Beethoven's symphonies. A hit with critics and audiences alike, it earned Dudamel an ECHO Award for New Artist of the Year from the German music industry. Also in 2005, he was selected as a last-minute replacement for the famous conductor Neeme Järvi for a well-received concert at London's Royal Albert Hall.

Dudamel's reputation continued to spread around the world over the next couple of years. He was awarded the 2006 Pegasus Prize at the Festival dei due monde (Festival of Two Worlds) in Spoleto, Italy. The festival jury claimed that they chose him due to his "talent, his conducting style, and for the indelible memory that his extraordinary concert left in the memory of the festival." He received more good news when Sweden's national orchestra, the Gothenburg Symphony, hired him as their principal conductor for the 2007-08 season. Having previously performed with the orchestra, he was delighted to commit to a schedule with them. "When I first conducted the Gothenburg Symphony ... last year, I was very impressed by their skill and openness," he said. "It was wonderful—I simply fell in love with the orchestra!"

Never one to shy away from work, Dudamel was able to balance his Gothenburg appointment with his duties as the leader of the SBYOV, to which he has remained very loyal. As Edward Smith, the chief executive of the Gothenburg Symphony, told the *Los Angeles Times*: "Every day that he's out of Caracas I think he feels that he should be there. It's not a duty; it's a passion, it's a religion." To top it off, he was offered a spot as a guest conductor with the Chicago Symphony Orchestra. Those around him took note of his frantic schedule. "He said to me the other day he wishes there were 600 days in a year," Smith told the *Los Angeles Times*. "Of course, he's doing too much, by anybody's normal standard, and I think he's beginning to realize it. But what is too much for Gustavo? What might be too much for an ordinary guy isn't too much for Gustavo." According to his manager, Mike Newbanks, "The problem with Gustavo is just simply one of demand, that so many people want to work with him." Dudamel's hard work continued to pay off when he received the 2007 Premio de la latinidad, an award given by the Union Latina for outstanding contributions to Latin cultural life.

Appreciation of Dudamel's work grew during his 2007 North American tour, as he wowed audiences with his exuberance, passion, and talent. Critics were impressed, comparing his charisma to that of conducting legend Leonard Bernstein. *New York Magazine* deemed his debut at New York's Carnegie Hall with the SBYOV the best performance of the year. The excitement building around him prompted the *Los Angeles Times* to coin the term "Dudamelmania" to describe it all. As the *Boston Globe* put it: "Dudamel and [the SBYOV] are now officially the most exciting thing in classical music. Over the last year or so, the excitement surrounding the frizzy-haired Dudamel has blossomed into all-out frenzy.... Rarely has one musician's potential seemed so limitless." His fellow musicians were impressed as well. "With Gustavo, the chops are all there," raved violinist Gil Shaham in *Newsweek.* "The technique, the mastery—he has it all."

Ever the professional, Dudamel does not let the pressure of media attention or high-profile events affect him. "I don't feel nervous in front of any orchestra," he shared. "I feel only excitement, adrenalin, pleasure. I love to conduct. It's what I was born to do. It's what I have done all my life."

> "*Dudamel and [the SBYOV] are now officially the most exciting thing in classical music. Over the last year or so, the excitement surrounding the frizzy-haired Dudamel has blossomed into all-out frenzy," said a reviewer for the* **Boston Globe**. *"Rarely has one musician's potential seemed so limitless."*

Worldwide Accolades and Media Appearances

Dudamel soon earned even more praise, receiving the 2007 Young Artists Award from the Royal Philharmonic Society in Great Britain and, along with Abreu, the 2008 "Q" Prize for extraordinary advocacy on behalf of children from the Harvard University School of Public Health. Also in 2008, the SBYOV won the Prince of Asturias Award for the Arts and recorded an album of Latin American musical pieces called *FIESTA*. His first performance with the Berlin Philharmonic at the Berlin Waldbühne, one of Europe's largest concert venues, was broadcast on German television that same year.

In addition, Director Enrique Sánchez Lansch filmed a documentary about Dudamel and the SBYOV called *The Promise of Music*. Released in 2008, the film follows the maestro and orchestra as they ready themselves for a concert at Beethovenfest in Bonn, Germany. By showcasing both the historical development of the SBYOV as well as their triumphant performance at Bonn, *The Promise of Music* illustrates the power of music to change lives.

As Dudamel took on new challenges over the years, he maintained his connection with SBYOV, shown here at a 2004 performance at Boston's Symphony Hall.

Dudamel achieved another first in 2008 when a recording of his performance of Hector Berlioz's *Symphonie fantastiqe* topped the *Billboard* classical chart. The following year, the French government named him a Chevalier dans l'ordre des arts et des lettres, one of the country's highest honors. In recognition of his many accomplishments and his meteoric rise to fame, *Time* magazine named him one of the 100 most influential people of 2009.

While Dudamel has enjoyed the attention and the new experiences that come with it, he has not allowed outside pressures to detract from what music really means to him. "It's only to have fun. This is the secret," he emphasized. "When you are sitting there, you need to have fun. Enjoy each moment. If your feelings are a little bit sad, you have to be there, to get it with the happy people. And all this energy." He has also recognized that being a professional is not the same thing as being a perfectionist. When asked if it mattered to him whether a performance was flawless, he responded, "I don't care. Even if it's not perfect, it's more about,'Wow. I will remember this forever.'"

Leading the Los Angeles Philharmonic

When Esa-Pekka Salonen was preparing to step down as the leader of the Los Angeles Philharmonic, Dudamel was tapped to take his place. In fact, the organization was so excited about hiring the young conductor that it did

Dudamel has developed a warm relationship with members of the Los Angeles Philharmonic, where he became music director in 2009.

not consider any other candidates and announced its transition plan two-and-a-half years in advance. The city of Los Angeles welcomed Dudamel with open arms, posting billboards and banners announcing his arrival and presenting a fireworks display in his honor. "He's a genuine star," former movie executive and University of Southern California professor Martin Kaplan proclaimed in the *New York Times*. "He's young. He has amazing hair. He has a great back story. He has a fantastic name. He's the dude!"

Commenting on the news, Salonen said, "The right successor has been found. Gustavo Dudamel's remarkable talent, intelligence, and energy are the absolute right match for the orchestra and Los Angeles. I am peaceful and joyous about the artist to whom we will pass the baton. There could not be a more forward looking choice." In turn, Dudamel expressed his gratitude. "I am honored to be chosen to succeed the great conductor/composer Esa-Pekka Salonen, who has given me so much support," he stated. "Playing with the Philharmonic in the magnificent Walt Disney Concert Hall is a great privilege, and I look forward to many happy years together."

On October 3, 2009, Dudamel began his inaugural season as the Los Angeles Philharmonic's music director with an event called *¡Bienvenido Gusta-*

vo!, a daylong musical celebration. The sold-out program included a variety of music—including gospel, jazz, pop, and blues—and culminated with Dudamel conducting Beethoven's Ninth Symphony. Five days later, he led the Los Angeles Philharmonic in the world premiere of composer John Adams's *City Noir* and a performance of Mahler's Symphony no. 1 at the Walt Disney Concert Hall. The entire event was broadcast on PBS and issued on DVD by Deutsche Grammophon.

Overall, the musicians of the Philharmonic greeted Dudamel warmly, sharing in the audience's enthusiasm for the young conductor. They expressed admiration for the maestro's technical know-how and his impressive ability to seduce, inspire, and lead the orchestra despite his young age. "It was noticeable from the very first rehearsal that Gustavo was paying a lot of attention not only to the string sound and intensity of expression, but to how the sound is produced," violinist Mark Kashper commented in the magazine *Strings.* As violist Dana Hansen explained on National Public Radio's "Morning Edition": "He looks young on the podium, but he doesn't act young. I've never heard of anyone conducting as much as he has in his young life." Clarinetist David Howard added, "If you look at what this man has to offer musically, it's really independent of his age."

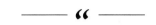

"I don't feel nervous in front of any orchestra," Dudamel shared. "I feel only excitement, adrenalin, pleasure. I love to conduct. It's what I was born to do. It's what I have done all my life."

During the 2009-10 season, Dudamel launched YOLA: Youth Orchestra Los Angeles, an initiative to provide underserved communities with access to exceptional music education, a program he modeled after Venezuela's *El Sistema*. He also directed the Los Angeles Philharmonic in the *Americas and Americans* festival, a series of concerts celebrating the cultural and musical traditions of North, Central, and South America. In addition to his work in Los Angeles, he has continued to conduct the Gothenburg Symphony and lead the SBYOV. In May 2010 he embarked on a coast-to-coast U.S. tour with the Los Angeles Philharmonic.

In Los Angeles, a city that emphasizes celebrity, Dudamel has become a superstar. When asked what it meant to have classical music become so popular, he had this to say. "If you're famous, you have to use your image for the other people," he stressed. "If I have the opportunity to be famous now, I want to show the kids and the new generation that it's possible—

*Dudamel at a rehearsal of YOLA (Youth Orchestra Los Angeles),
which he formed to provide music education to children who might not
otherwise have the opportunity.*

it's possible to make it to reality, that you can have a career, be successful, enjoy.… And now to bring this orchestra to the people who don't have the opportunity to have classical music. It's really important—one of the most important things. Because that is *our* future, and we have to be in the future. Especially here in L.A.—especially in my home."

MARRIAGE AND FAMILY

In 2006, Dudamel married Eloísa Maturén, a ballet dancer, choreographer, and journalist. As his workload and fame continued to increase, she helped her husband make artistic decisions and served as his translator while he was learning English. Gothenburg Symphony's Edward Smith told the *Los Angeles Times* that Maturén "will say things to Gustavo, usually in Spanish, extraordinarily perceptive things about a performance or a performer that [others may] feel more inhibited" about expressing. After Dudamel became conductor of the Los Angeles Philharmonic, the couple moved to the Hollywood Hills to start a new life. "This is a great time for him to slow down a bit and spend some more time with his wife," his manager Mark Newbanks commented in the *Los Angeles Times*. "They love to cook together, they love to read together, they love to listen to music together, they love to dance together."

Dudamel has claimed that things have worked well between him and his wife ever since they first met. "Eloísa came in the right time in my life," he said. "She came when I won the competition in Bamberg, and all the big orchestras were starting to call me, you know.… I was conducting a lot in Venezuela, but I started to do more traveling around with different orchestras. And when she arrived in my life, it was like, 'Wow.'" He has told the press that he hopes to have "a big, big family" someday.

HOBBIES AND OTHER INTERESTS

Although his first passion is classical music, Dudamel enjoys listening to a wide variety of other styles. "I love, of course, Latin music—salsa, merengue, boleros," he explained. "I love Beatles, Pink Floyd, Led Zeppelin. It's amazing! I can speak to you a lot in the way of pop music." He's also a big fan of Los Angeles's local eateries. "I love hot dogs," he admitted. "They made a hot dog for me, with my name, at Pink's [a famous L.A. hotdog stand], with jalapeño, guacamole, nachos, everything. It's not very Venezuelan, it's more Mexican. But it doesn't matter. I love to eat." He also enjoys playing soccer, swimming, and watching the L.A. Lakers.

RECORDINGS

Ludwig van Beethoven: Symphonies nos. 5 & 7, 2006 (with the Simón Bolívar Youth Orchestra of Venezuela)

Béla Bartók: Concerto for Orchestra, 2007 (with the Los Angeles Philharmonic)

Birthday Concert for Pope Benedict XVI, 2007 (DVD)

Gustav Mahler: Symphony no. 5, 2007 (with the Simón Bolívar Youth Orchestra of Venezuela)

FIESTA, 2008 (with the Simón Bolívar Youth Orchestra of Venezuela)

Hector Berlioz: Symphonie fantastique, 2008 (with the Los Angeles Philharmonic)

The Promise of Music, 2008 (DVD)

El Sistema: Music to Change Life, 2009 (DVD)

Gustavo Dudamel and the Los Angeles Philharmonic: The Inaugural Concert, 2009 (DVD)

HONORS AND AWARDS

Bamberger Symphoniker Gustav Mahler Conducting Competition: 2004, Winner

Pegasus Prize (Festival dei due monde, Italy): 2006

Classic FM Gramophone Award: 2007, WQXR Gramophone Special Recognition Award (with the Simón Bolívar Youth Orchestra of Venezuela)

Culture Award (*New York Magazine*): 2007, Best Performance of the Year, for debut at Carnegie Hall with the Simón Bolívar Youth Orchestra of Venezuela

ECHO Award (German Recording Industry): 2007, New Artist of the Year

Premio de la latinidad (Union Latina): 2007, for outstanding contributions to Latin cultural life

Young Artists Award (Royal Philharmonic Society, Great Britain): 2007

City of Toronto Glenn Gould Protégé Prize (Glenn Gould Foundation): 2008

Prince of Asturias Award for the Arts (Spain): 2008 (with the Simón Bolívar Youth Orchestra of Venezuela)

"Q" Prize (Harvard University School of Public Health): 2008, for extraordinary advocacy on behalf of children (with Dr. José Antonio Abreu)

Chevalier dans l'ordre des arts et des lettres (France): 2009

100 Most Influential People (*Time* magazine): 2009

Eugene McDermott Award in the Arts (Massachusetts Institute of Technology): 2010

FURTHER READING

Periodicals

BBC Music Magazine, June 2008, p.24

Gramophone, Nov. 2006, p.25

Los Angeles Times, Dec. 31, 2006, p.F1; Apr. 11, 2007, p.E1

Los Angeles Times Magazine, Aug. 8, 2009, p.28

New York Times, Nov. 13, 2009, p.A1; Nov. 22, 2009, p.23

New Yorker, Dec. 14, 2009, p.90

Newsweek, Jan. 7, 2008, p.92

Vogue, Sep. 2009, p.518

Online Articles

http://www.boston.com
   (Boston Globe, "The Maestro at 25: Venezuelan Conductor Gustavo Dudamel Has Had a Meteoric Rise to Prominence," Aug. 25, 2006)

http://www.latimes.com
   (Los Angeles Times, "Gustavo Dudamel Learns to Conduct His Career," Sep. 26, 2009)

http://www.latimes.com
   (Los Angeles Times Magazine, "Gustavo Dudamel: Passion Play," Aug. 2009)

http://www.npr.org
(National Public Radio Morning Edition, "Dudamel Leads L.A. Philharmonic in Concert," Oct. 8, 2009)
http://www.nytimes.com
(New York Times, "The Kid's Got Energy. Now Watch Him Conduct," Nov. 30, 2007)
http://www.nytimes.com
(New York Times Magazine, "Conductor of the People," Oct. 28, 2007)
http://www.topics.nytimes.com
(New York Times, "Gustavo Dudamel," various articles, multiple dates)
http://www.cbsnews.com
(60 Minutes, "Gustavo the Great," Feb. 17, 2008)
http://www.time.com
(Time Magazine, "Gustavo Dudamel," May 11, 2009)
http://entertainment.timesonline.co.uk
(Times Online, "True Class: South America's Lightning Conductor," Feb. 15, 2007)

ADDRESS

Gustavo Dudamel
Los Angeles Philharmonic
151 South Grand Avenue
Los Angeles, CA 90012-3034

WORLD WIDE WEB SITES

http://www.gustavodudamel.com
http://elsistemausa.org
http://www.laphil.com/gustavo/index.html
http://vadimrepin.com/artistmicrosite/DUDGU/en/index.htms
http://www.fesnojiv.gob.ve/en.html

Tavi Gevinson 1996-

American Fashion Blogger
Creator of the Blog "Style Rookie"

EARLY YEARS

Tavi Gevinson was born on April 22, 1996. She is the youngest of three daughters born to Steve Gevinson and Berit Engen. They live in the western suburbs of Chicago, Illinois. Her mother is an artist, and her father teaches English at a high school in Oak Park, Illinois. Gevinson and her two sisters learned to speak Norwegian from their mother, who is originally from Oslo, Norway. Although she can't speak the language as well as she could when she was younger, Tavi says that she knows "enough to get by and travel."

MAJOR ACCOMPLISHMENTS

Starting the "Style Rookie" Blog

Gevinson is currently a high school student in the Chicago area. She has become famous in the world of high fashion for a blog that she started writing when she was only 11 years old. She first started getting interested in fashion in early 2008. "Before then I just dressed for comfort," she said. "I was more into just a T-shirt and jeans or pajama pants. Practicality and comfort." Then, a friend's teenage sister started a blog that discussed fashion trends and featured photos of herself. This sparked Gevinson's interest. She began reading *Seventeen* magazine and watching the television show "America's Next Top Model" to soak up more fashion facts and ideas.

> *Gevinson's first post began simply: "Well I am new here.... Lately I've been really interested in fashion, and I like to make binders and slideshows of 'high-fashion' modeling and designs. I'd like to know of neat websites and magazines, so comments are welcome. I plan on posting pictures in the future, but for now, I'm just getting started. Yours truly, Tavi."*

On March 31, 2008, Gevinson made her first post to her blog, originally called "Style Rookie/New Girl in Town" and later changed to simply "Style Rookie." She started out using the name Tavi Williams, but she now identifies herself with her real name, or "Tavi G." Her first post began simply: "Well I am new here.... Lately I've been really interested in fashion, and I like to make binders and slideshows of 'high-fashion' modeling and designs. I'd like to know of neat websites and magazines, so comments are welcome. I plan on posting pictures in the future, but for now, I'm just getting started. Yours truly, Tavi." She was just 11 years old when she made that first post.

As Gevinson became more interested in fashion, she began to dress in a unique and offbeat personal style. Her approach to fashion sometimes attracted the attention of her middle school classmates, many of whom weren't aware that she was writing a fashion blog. "Not that many know about it," she commented. "My closest [friends] do, but it's embarrassing to talk about." She was really happy the day a classmate said "I watch your outfits every day; it's like something new and I'm excited to see it." Gevinson relished the compliment. "He doesn't know about my blog. Some people at my school who know about my blog and then compliment my outfits a lot but it's like, before they knew about my blog, they sort of like snorted at them. So I know it's more sincere, coming from him, because he doesn't know about it."

As her blog developed, Gevinson developed a writing style that was youthful, yet insightful and sophisticated. She found writing for her blog a totally new experience, one she enjoyed. "I never really liked writing before because at school I never got to write about what I like," she admitted. "With my blog, it's my thoughts, like my brain is being translated onto the computer." In addition to writing, she also included pictures of styles that interested her, and pictures of herself in outfits she put together. For the most part, she took these herself, using a Canon Powershot A590IS. She says this "takes good pictures but is still easy to use." With an old tripod of her dad's to hold the camera in place and a self-timer button, she was easily able to photograph herself. When finished, she uploaded them to her computer, sometimes using PhotoFiltre software to create special effects.

"I never really liked writing before because at school I never got to write about what I like," Gevinson admitted. "With my blog, it's my thoughts, like my brain is being translated onto the computer."

In the beginning, her posts typically only drew a few comments from readers, but that soon changed. Gevinson hadn't asked her parents' permission when she started her blog—something she now says was irresponsible. Her father only became fully aware of his daughter's blog when she had to ask his permission to be featured in an article in the *New York Times Style Magazine* about teenage fashion bloggers. At 12 years old, Gevinson was the youngest person mentioned in the article.

Backlash Begins

As Gevinson's name began to be heard around the fashion world, some people began questioning if her blog was really her own work. Her writing voice at times sounded very mature, and her thoughts about

Gevinson sitting at home amongst the fashion magazine clippings she's using to make a collage for her blog.

the fashion world were certainly more insightful than what anyone would expect from a girl her age. Some influential columnists suggested that there was really a "Team Tavi" and that the blog was the work of several people older than her. Furthermore, it was suggested that even if the blog really was put together by Gevinson, it was ridiculous to give so much attention to the thoughts of a middle school student, and the only reason her blog drew attention was because she was very young, and therefore a novelty. Anne Slowey, an editor of *Elle* magazine, and Lesley M.M. Blume, a fashion writer, were especially harsh in their comments.

For Gevinson, it was upsetting to have her work called into question like that. She defended herself by saying: "No one in my family helps me with my writing, outfits, videos, or pictures (they have offered now and then for the pictures but I guess it's kind of embarrassing for me so I refused)." Answering her critics in one of her blog posts, she said, "I will agree with the fact that I'm 12 shouldn't set me apart from other bloggers, and it definitely shouldn't play a part in how one might react to how I think or write or dress." She found the whole issue "really annoying" and commented that "People complain that my generation is stupid, but when I show that I have a brain, they call me a fake."

Gevinson continued to pursue and develop her interests in fashion and blogging despite her critics. She was getting plenty of positive publicity, too. For example, *Teen Vogue* published an interview with her and praised "her dead-on style observations and fearless fashion sense that puts even the most daring fashionistas to shame." The number of daily hits on her blog was climbing steadily, reaching about 30,000 hits a day.

Gevinson's Inspirations

To get inspiration for her blog, Gevinson visits other fashion blogs and Web sites from around the world. Even though she can't read all the languages, the visual nature of fashion makes that less important. Among her favorite designers are Rei Kawakubo, Yohji Yamamoto, Vivienne Westwood, Kate and Laura Mulleavy, Tao Kurihara, Alexander McQueen, and Luella Bartley.

She has also formed friendships with other like-minded bloggers. "It's pretty cool how global the fashion blogging community is," she noted. She likes to look at old and new fashion magazines, including *Sassy, Lula, Vogue, Numero,* and *Dazed and Confused.* Ideas also come from "photography (fashion and otherwise), movies, fine art, books, plays, street style, runway, music, hobos, celebrities … it changes a lot," she said. "Though I don't think I will ever tire of Japanese street style, the 70's, or evil fairy tale creatures."

Ideas and inspiration come from "photography (fashion and otherwise), movies, fine art, books, plays, street style, runway, music, hobos, celebrities … it changes a lot," Gevinson remarked. "Though I don't think I will ever tire of Japanese street style, the 70's, or evil fairy tale creatures."

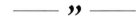

Small in stature, Gevinson has described herself as "a tiny 13-year-old dork that sits inside all day." She doesn't like to give her personal style a name. "It's still developing and evolving, and phrases and labels like 'hippie chic' bother me. I think giving it a description would tie me down too much, I'm still experimenting after all." Since becoming well-known, she has received gifts of clothing from many designers, but she also creates her outfits with items from her local thrift shop, hand-me-downs, and even the box of dress-up clothes she and her sisters played with when they were younger. She shops with money from her allowance and babysitting jobs. She doesn't sew, claiming that she might like to learn how but also admitting that she might not have the patience.

Fashion Connections and International Travel

The Internet has made it possible for Gevinson to reach millions of readers and to follow fashion trends in places far from her home, all without leaving her hometown in the Midwest. Her blog has also provided her with some incredible opportunities to travel the world. In September 2009, not long after she appeared on the cover of the trendy magazine *Pop* and was also featured in the fashion publication *Love,* Gevinson went to New York City with her father to attend a week of fashion events known as Fashion Week. There she was able to see the latest collections and meet some of her inspirations.

One such opportunity came from Kate and Laura Mulleavy, two sisters who design for the Rodarte fashion house. Once they discovered Gevinson's blog, they got in touch with her, even sending her a pair of hand-knitted tights from their collection. The relationship grew, and the sisters eventually gave Gevinson a personal invitation to one of their shows. Late in 2009, the Mulleavys launched a new clothing line in cooperation with the Target chain of stores. The pieces in the collection were inspired by Gevinson, who also starred in the promotional video shot for the line. "Tavi makes you think about things differently, makes you see things differently," said Kate Mulleavy.

Gevinson holds designer Rei Kawakubo of Comme des Garcons in such high esteem that in November 2008, she wrote a rap tribute to the designer and posted it on her blog and on the Web site Vimeo, where it got hundreds of hits. The following November, she was invited to Tokyo to be the guest of honor at the Comme des Garcons holiday party. Gevinson attended with her mother, and also had a series of photo shoots with Japanese magazines while she was there.

The following January, Gevinson and her father flew to Paris to see the spring fashion collections there, and in February they were in New York for more shows. She became the youngest person ever to contribute to *Harper's Bazaar* when she was asked to write up her impressions of some of the spring collections for the magazine's January 2010 issue. These travels led to more criticism for her family, as some columnists expressed the opinion that a girl of her age shouldn't be missing school to attend fashion events. Such comments irked Gevinson, who replied, "My parents and I are the ones who know my school's absences policy, how my teachers feel about my missing school, and what my grades look like—not anyone else."

A 2010 runway show featuring creations by Japanese designer Rei Kawakubo for Comme des Garcons, one of Gevinson's favorite designers.

Throughout her travels, Gevinson has continued to focus on her "Style Rookie" blog. Estimates of how many people regularly check in with her blog range from one to four million. Still, she says she simply does it because it is fun. She likes "getting dressed and taking pictures and rambling on about fantastic editorials and runway collections," but says she will give it up if it starts to have a negative impact on her grades at school. "I'm here to develop my style and be able to converse with other bloggers that share my love for fashion," she stated.

> "Wear what you want, write about things that you care about, and just have fun with it," Gevinson advised those interested in blogging. "It's easy to tell when someone is trying too hard to impress readers and get more comments, and it's kind of a turnoff." For those interested in creating their own personal style, she said, "Dress however you please and embrace rude stares. It means that what you're wearing isn't boring!"

Future Plans

Gevinson doesn't really see herself pursuing a career in fashion, but says she isn't sure yet what she will do with her future. She has lots of ideas. "I would like to go to school, then have a band, then have a magazine where I could photograph/art direct/write, then write and direct and maybe act in the movies, then write and direct and maybe act on stage, then be an elementary school teacher, then write again, then move to the woods."

To anyone who might be interested in blogging about fashion, Gevinson had this advice: "Wear what you want, write about things that you care about, and just have fun with it. It's easy to tell when someone is trying too hard to impress readers and get more comments, and it's kind of a turnoff." For those interested in creating their own personal style, she said: "Dress however you please and embrace rude stares. It means that what you're wearing isn't boring!"

HOME AND FAMILY

Gevinson said there wasn't anyone else in her family particularly interested in fashion, although her mother sometimes wears "strange things, like painted harem pants and purple tie-dye leggings. She likes dressing up but isn't into fashion like a blogger is, and still doesn't understand some of my outfits. My dad dresses like dads dress." In general, her parents don't

Gevinson at the Marc Jacobs Fall 2010 collection,
showing off her unique sense of style.

read her blog much, but they are "very supportive," she said. "Sometimes I'll show them a post or two especially if I'm proud of it or something. They think it's crazy, some of the things that have come out of it, but they're happy that I have fun with it."

FAVORITE BOOKS AND MUSIC

Gevinson's favorite musician is Bob Dylan. Her favorite band is Wilco. She also likes many other bands and artists, including Neutral Milk Hotel, Cat Power, Pete Seeger, Joni Mitchell, Frank Sinatra, Joan Baez, and Feist.

Some of her favorite books are *The Westing Game* by Ellen Raskin, *Arthur and the True Francine* by Marc Brown, *The Lorax* by Dr. Seuss, *The Five People You Meet in Heaven* by Mitch Albom, and *Walk Two Moons* by Sharon Creech.

HOBBIES AND OTHER INTERESTS

Gevinson enjoys sledding with her friends, reading, writing, playing guitar, riding her bike, singing, and acting. She has been in several musicals, including *Thoroughly Modern Millie, Beauty and the Beast, Seussical,* and *Once on This Island.*

FURTHER READING

Periodicals

Independent, Oct. 10, 2009, p.28
Times (London), Oct. 8, 2009, p. T2
Wall Street Journal, Sep. 11, 2009, p. W1

Online Articles

http://www.chicagotribune.com
   (Chicago Tribune, "Tavi Gevinson Earns Acclaim with Style Rookie
   Fashion Blog," Dec. 30, 2009)
http://www.dailymail.co.uk
   (Daily Mail, "Move over Geldof Girls: Meet Tavi, 13, the 'Tiny' Blogger
   with the Fashion Industry at Her Feet," Sep. 23, 2009)
http://thefashioninformer.typepad.com
   (Fashion Informer, "Random Questions for .... Tavi G," Feb. 4, 2010)
http://www.interviewmagazine.com
   (Interview, "Tavi Williams, Rookie of the Year," Mar. 13, 2009)
http://www.nytimes.com
   (New York Times, "Bloggers Crash Fashion's First Row," Dec. 24, 2009)

http://www.nytimes.com
   (New York Times Style Magazine, "Post Adolescents," Fall 2008)
http://www.teenvogue.com
   (Teen Vogue, "Tavi Gevinson defines Rodarte for Target," Nov. 11, 2009)
http://www.telegraph.co.uk
   (Telegraph, "Pre-Fall 2010 Heralds the Return of Classic Dressing,
   Brown Leather and Tavi Gevinson," Feb. 3, 2010)
http://www.timesonline.co.uk
   (The Times, "Tavi, the Tiny Fashion Blogger: Tavi Gevinson Is Fashion's
   New It Girl—and She's Only 13," Oct. 8, 2009)

ADDRESS

Tavi Gevinson
Biz 3 Publicity
1321 North Milwaukee Avenue #452
Chicago, IL 60642

WORLD WIDE WEB SITES

http://www.thestylerookie.com
http://tavi.thepop.com

LeBron James 1984-

American Professional Basketball Player with the
Miami Heat
Winner of the NBA's Most Valuable Player Award in
2008-09 and 2009-10

BIRTH

LeBron James was born on December 30, 1984, in Akron,
Ohio. He is the only child of Gloria James, who was 16 and
single at the time of his birth. His biological father, Anthony
McClelland, did not play a role in his upbringing. But LeBron
developed a close relationship with one of his mother's
boyfriends, Eddie Jackson, who lived with his family for a few

years during his childhood. He has referred to Jackson as his father on several occasions.

YOUTH

LeBron first became interested in basketball in 1987, when he received a toy ball and adjustable hoop for Christmas. Although it was still a few days before he reached his third birthday, he loved running toward the hoop, jumping, and dunking the ball. He kept dunking even as the adults in the house raised the height of the basket. "All he would do is start back from the living room, run through the dining room, and he was still dunking the ball," Jackson recalled. "I was thinking, 'Man, this kid has some elevation for just being three years old.'"

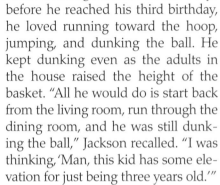

> *James became interested in basketball when he received an adjustable hoop when he was almost three. He kept dunking the ball, and the adults kept raising the hoop. "All he would do is start back from the living room, run through the dining room, and he was still dunking the ball," Jackson recalled. "I was thinking, 'Man, this kid has some elevation for just being three years old.'"*

Up to this time, LeBron and his mother had been living with his grandmother, Freda James, in an old Victorian house in Akron. But when his grandmother died, Gloria James was unable to maintain the residence. She was forced to move into a public housing project in Akron and raise LeBron as a single mother. Although Gloria James worked at several jobs, she often struggled to put food on the table and provide a stable home environment for her son. In fact, LeBron lived in a dozen different places between the ages of five and eight. "I just grabbed my little backpack, which held all the possessions I needed, and said to myself what I always said to myself: 'It's time to roll,'" he remembered.

Despite his unsettled home life, LeBron somehow managed to stay out of trouble. "You had gunshots flying and cop cars driving around there all the time," he acknowledged. "As a young boy, it was scary, but I never got into none of that stuff. That just wasn't me. I knew it was wrong." Still, the frequent moves caused him to miss a lot of school, including more than half of the fourth grade. Once he started playing organized basketball at the age of nine, however, he gained some stability by living with the family of

In his book, Shooting Stars, *James recounts his early experiences playing basketball and the close friendships he developed with his teammates.*

his coach, Frankie Walker. It was in Walker's home that LeBron experienced structure and discipline for the first time. "It changed my life," he stated. "The next year I had perfect attendance and a B average."

Practically from the first time he walked onto a basketball court, LeBron dominated other players with his unusual size, strength, athleticism, ball-handling skills, and passing ability. He played on a youth basketball team called the Shooting Stars and developed close relationships with several of his teammates, including Dru Joyce Jr., Sian Cotton, and Willie McGee. The Shooting Stars won more than 200 games and claimed several Amateur Athletic Union (AAU) championships over the next few years.

In 2009 LeBron published a book called *Shooting Stars* about his youth basketball experiences and his friendships with his teammates. His early playing days also became the subject of a 2009 documentary film called *More Than a Game.* "I believe that everything happens for a reason, and my struggles here in [Akron] helped to make me who I am," he declared. "My teammates and I got to see the light at the end of the tunnel. We all loved basketball, we all had the same goal, and when you have six or seven guys with that much in common, all staying on the right track, you can accomplish a lot."

EDUCATION

By the time he reached high school age, James was recognized as one of the most talented young players in Akron. Several area coaches tried to lure him to their schools. Many people assumed that he would attend Buchtel, a public high school in West Akron that James described as "the school of choice for skilled black athletes." But James had made a pact with his three best friends, Joyce, Cotton, and McGee. "We called ourselves the Fab Four," he recalled. "We decided we'd all go to the same school together. We promised that nothing would break us up—girls, coaches, basketball. We'd hang together no matter what."

When it became clear that Joyce would not make the varsity basketball team at Buchtel, all four boys decided to attend St. Vincent-St. Mary, a private, all-boys Catholic high school in Akron. Their decision to attend this predominantly white school shocked and disappointed some local fans. "The four of us may have been brothers to each other," James acknowledged. "But to many in Akron's black community, we were now traitors who had sold out to the white establishment." James and his friends also faced a rough transition when they started classes at St. Vincent-St. Mary, with its strict dress code and high academic standards. But their success on the basketball court soon swept away any doubts they may have had.

With James and his friends leading the varsity team as freshmen, the St. Vincent-St. Mary Fighting Irish posted a perfect 27-0 record during the 1999-2000 season to win the Division III Ohio state championship. James contributed 18.0 points and 6.2 rebounds per game that year. As a sophomore in 2000-01, he increased his scoring average to 25.2 points per game while adding 7.2 rebounds, 5.8 assists, and 3.8 steals. The Fighting Irish posted an impressive 27-1 record and claimed a second straight state title. James became the first sophomore in history to be named Mr. Basketball for the state of Ohio.

To the surprise of many people, James also played varsity football during his second year at St. Vincent-St. Mary. His height and leaping ability made him a natural at wide receiver. He caught 42 passes for 820 yards and 7 touchdowns that year and earned all-state honors. As a junior, he caught 61 passes for 1,245 yards and 16 touchdowns and led his team to the semifinals of the state tournament. "Football is my first love," James declared. "I still like football more than basketball." Unfortunately, an injury prevented him from playing football again as a senior.

In high school, James made a pact with his three best friends, Dru Joyce Jr., Sian Cotton, and Willie McGee. "We called ourselves the Fab Four," he recalled. "We decided we'd all go to the same school together. We promised that nothing would break us up—girls, coaches, basketball. We'd hang together no matter what."

Becoming a National Phenomenon

By the time his junior-year basketball season got underway, James was widely considered to be among the best young players in the country. He had dazzled both college and National Basketball Association (NBA) scouts with his dominating performances at high-profile summer basketball camps. Although James showed great scoring ability, experts also praised his maturity and court vision, which had the effect of making his teammates better. Some observers even compared him to NBA Hall of Fame players like Magic Johnson and Michael Jordan.

During the 2001-02 season, when James was a junior, he averaged 29.0 points, 8.3 rebounds, 5.7 assists, and 3.3 steals per game and claimed his second straight Ohio Mr. Basketball award. His remarkable skills attracted

*James playing for St. Vincent-St. Mary High School in 2003, his senior year.
The crowds were so big that the team had to play at college facilities
to accommodate the spectators.*

national attention. In February 2002 the 17-year-old James appeared on
the cover of *Sports Illustrated* under the caption "The Chosen One." The
accompanying article described him as a "basketball genius" and predicted
that he would be the first player selected in the NBA draft. Los Angeles
Lakers star Shaquille O'Neal showed up to watch one of his high school
games and stuck around to talk with the young star afterward. "He said I

was going to be good, and to keep up the good work," James remembered. "As a junior in high school at the time, that sticks with you."

All the hype created a distraction for James and his teammates, however, and they fell short in their pursuit of a third consecutive state championship. "We didn't respect the game of basketball," he admitted. "When we got to the last game of the season, the championship, we got beat." But the heartbreaking loss helped them put things in perspective and get back on track for the following year. "We rededicated ourselves to the game, we approached the game the right way, and good karma came back to us," James noted.

During James's senior season in 2002-03, the Fighting Irish had to play their home games at the University of Akron in order to accommodate the crowds that wanted to see him play. Several St. Vincent-St. Mary games were nationally televised on cable sports network ESPN. "Now that I look back on it, I'm like, 'Wow, that was huge,'" James stated. "We were one of the first [high school teams] to start it all up, doing nationally televised games, traveling the U.S., taking planes to big tournaments." James lived up to the high expectations by averaging 31.6 points, 9.6 rebounds, 4.6 assists, and 3.4 steals per game. He led his team to a 25-1 record and another state title, as well as the *USA Today* National High School Championship.

James received a number of prestigious honors at the conclusion of his senior season. He claimed his third Mr. Basketball award, was named the national High School Player of the Year by *Parade Magazine* and *USA Today,* and was honored as a McDonald's High School All-American. Shortly before James graduated from St. Vincent-St. Mary in the spring of 2003, he announced that he would forego college basketball and make himself eligible for the NBA draft. Although few people doubted that he had the talent to play in the NBA, his decision generated a great deal of debate. Some people questioned the wisdom of NBA rules allowing young players to skip college and turn professional straight out of high school. They claimed that playing college basketball helped young players mature and gave them tools to make better decisions about their future.

To support this claim, critics pointed to some questionable decisions that had been made by James and his family. For example, Gloria James bought her son an $80,000 Hummer sport-utility vehicle—complete with built-in TV screens and a custom leather interior embossed with his nickname, "King James"—as an early graduation present. Since her struggles as a single mother were well known, many people wondered how she could afford such a lavish gift. Some speculated that James had violated the rules that prohibited amateur athletes from accepting money or gifts based on their potential future earnings and marketability. Following an investigation, the Ohio High School Athletic Association ruled the vehicle acceptable since Gloria James had obtained loans to purchase it. But the investigators suspended James for one game for improperly accepting two vintage jerseys worth an estimated $850 from a Cleveland store owner.

CAREER HIGHLIGHTS

NBA—The Cleveland Cavaliers

The controversy surrounding James's finances ended when he was selected as the top pick in the 2003 NBA draft by the Cleveland Cavaliers. He signed a four-year, $18.8 million contract with the team. He also arranged several major endorsement deals with large companies, including a seven-year, $90 million contract with Nike that was believed to be the most lucrative ever awarded to an athlete. At the age of 19, James was expected to resurrect the Cavaliers franchise—which had posted a dismal 17-65 record the previous year—and bring new fans and energy to the NBA. He remained calm under the intense pressure and expressed confidence in his ability to turn his hometown team into a contender. "This is going to be great," he stated. "We're finally going to get more life in this city."

"I just wanted to be on the Olympic team and have the experience," James said after the 2004 Olympics. "Everything on the court I did not expect, but I think I'd do it again."

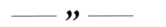

During his rookie season in 2003-04, James somehow managed to exceed the high expectations that had greeted his arrival in the NBA. He put the league on notice by scoring 25 points and handing out 9 assists in his first professional game. He went on to start 79 games that season and average 20.9 points, 5.5 rebounds, 5.9 assists, and 1.65 steals per game. During a game against the New Jersey Nets in March 2004, he scored 41 points to become the youngest player ever to score more than 40 in a game. James's strong performance helped the Cavs double their number of victories from the previous season to finish with a 35-47 record. Although Cleveland missed the playoffs by one game, James easily claimed the NBA Rookie of the Year award.

During the 2004 offseason, James became the youngest male basketball player ever to compete in the Summer Olympic Games. As a member of

Airborn in 2004, winding up for a breakaway dunk against the Los Angeles Lakers.

Team USA, he joined a group of fellow NBA stars that included Allen Iverson, Carmelo Anthony, and Tim Duncan. The American "Dream Team" arrived in Athens, Greece, as heavy favorites to win the gold medal. After all, Team USA had earned an impressive 109-2 record against international competition and won three Olympic gold medals since the United States first allowed professional basketball players to compete in 1992. Limited practice time and internal bickering made it difficult for the 2004 players to come together as a team, however, and the Americans had to settle for a bronze medal. "I just wanted to be on the Olympic team and have the experience," James said afterward. "Everything on the court I did not expect, but I think I'd do it again."

James continued to prove he belonged in the NBA during the 2004-05 season. He scored 56 points during a game against the Toronto Raptors to become the youngest player ever to score more than 50 in a game. He was also named a starter on the NBA All-Star Team. In just his second NBA season, James ranked third in the league in scoring with an average of 27.2 points per game, while adding 7.0 rebounds, 7.2 assists, and 2.21 steals. The Cavs started the season strong with a 31-21 record, but then spiraled downward to post an 11-19 record over the last 30 games. Although Cleveland achieved its first winning record since 1998 at 42-40, the Cavs failed to make the playoffs. Some observers argued that James needed to speak up and take more of a leadership role if he hoped to lead the Cavs into the postseason.

Leading His Team to the Playoffs

During the 2005-06 season James emerged as one of the most dominant players in the NBA. Appearing in just his second All-Star Game, he scored 29 points and became the youngest player ever to be named the contest's Most Valuable Player. He went on to post amazing season averages of 31.4 points, 7.0 rebounds, 6.6 assists, and 1.56 steals per game. With James leading the way, the Cavs posted an impressive 50-32 record to finish second in the Central Division of the Eastern Conference and earn a spot in the playoffs. The Cavs defeated the Washington Wizards in the first round, but lost a tough, seven-game series to the Detroit Pistons in the conference semifinals.

At the conclusion of the 2006 season, the 21-year-old James surprised many observers by firing his agent and forming his own company, LRMR Marketing, with three of his longtime friends. Although the foursome lacked business experience, they hired top-notch lawyers and accountants to assist them. James also made friends with billionaire investor Warren Buffett, who

James led his team to the 2007 Eastern Conference Finals, where they beat the Detroit Pistons in six games to reach the NBA Finals for the first time in franchise history. Here, James is pressured by Chris Webber (84) and Tayshaun Prince (22).

provided him with financial advice. James and his colleagues negotiated a three-year, $10.8 million contract extension with the Cavaliers. His NBA salary made up just a small portion of his overall earnings, however, which included more than $100 million in endorsement deals with Nike, Sprite, Powerade, Upper Deck, Bubblicious, and other companies.

In James's fourth pro season in 2006-07, he became the undisputed leader of his team, both on the court and in the locker room. He made his third consecutive appearance in the All-Star Game and scored 28 points for the Eastern Conference team. Posting season averages of 27.3 points, 6.7 rebounds, 6.0 assists, and 1.6 steals per game, James led the Cavs to another 50-32 record and second place finish in the division. Cleveland knocked out the Washington Wizards in the first round of the playoffs, then beat the New Jersey Nets in the second round to advance to the Eastern Conference Finals.

James and his teammates faced the Detroit Pistons, a tough, playoff-seasoned team full of talented veterans. Few people believed that the relatively inexperienced Cavs could prevail in a seven-game playoff series. The Pistons won the first two games, but Cleveland surprised many fans by coming back to win the next two. In Game 5, James turned in what broadcaster Marv Albert described as "one of the all-time performances in NBA history." He was an unstoppable force on the court, scoring 48 points—including 29 of his team's last 30—to lift the Cavs to victory in a double-overtime thriller. "That was the single best game I've ever seen at this level in this atmosphere, hands down," Cleveland Coach Mike Brown said afterward. The Cavaliers went on to eliminate the Pistons in six games to reach the NBA Finals for the first time in franchise history. James could not re-create the magic in the Finals, however, and the Cavs were swept in four games by the San Antonio Spurs.

> ❝
>
> *"It's hard for me to congratulate somebody after you just lose to them," James conceded. "I'm a winner. It's not being a poor sport or anything like that. If somebody beats you up, you're not going to congratulate them. That doesn't make sense to me. I'm a competitor."*
>
> ❞

James had another outstanding season in 2007-08. He became the youngest player in NBA history to score 10,000 career points, surpassed 10,389 points to become the Cavaliers' all-time leading scorer, and scored 27 points to be named Most Valuable Player of the All-Star Game. James also led the NBA in scoring average with 30.0 points per game, while adding 7.9 rebounds, 7.2 assists, and 1.8 steals. The Cavs struggled with injuries to key players for part of the season, then made a big trade in February to bring in such veteran players as Ben Wallace, Joe Smith, Wally Szczerbiak, and Delonte West. Although Cleveland finished the season with a 45-37 record, the Cavs seemed well-positioned to make some noise in the playoffs.

After eliminating the Washington Wizards in the first round, the Cavs faced the Boston Celtics in the Eastern Conference Semifinals. In a grueling playoff series, the two teams battled to a 3-3 tie. The deciding Game 7 turned into a scoring duel between James and Celtics veteran Paul Pierce. Although James outscored Pierce 45-41, the Celtics prevailed and went on to win the NBA title. "I did everything I could to get us over the hump," James said afterward. "Paul Pierce made some spectacular plays. He just willed his team to victory."

Although his fifth pro season ended in disappointment, James was determined to continue improving his game. "We had a great season, but I knew that I could get better, and I took it as a challenge to get better," he stated. "In the summer I dedicated myself to working hard so I could come in and be successful every night." Part of his summer workout regimen included playing in the 2008 Summer Olympic Games in Beijing, China. James joined an American team that had undergone major changes following the embarrassment of 2004. Team USA coaches took their time in selecting a roster of players who would work well together, then made sure that they got plenty of practice as a team. The changes paid off, as the American "Redeem Team" won all eight games in the Olympic tournament in convincing fashion to bring home a gold medal.

Earning MVP Honors

Over the course of the 2008-09 season, James "catapulted himself from among the elite of today's NBA players into the mix of all-time greats," according to Sean Deveney of *Sporting News.* He played in his fifth consecutive All-Star Game, shot a career high .489 from the field and .780 from the free-throw line, and led the NBA with seven triple-doubles (games in which he posted double-digit numbers in three statistical categories). James's stellar season averages of 28.4 points, 7.6 rebounds, 7.2 assists, and 1.69 steals per game helped him earn the NBA's Most Valuable Player Award.

James led the Cavaliers to a league-best 66-16 record to earn the top seed in the playoffs. Cleveland swept past the Detroit Pistons and the Atlanta Hawks in the first two rounds to reach the Eastern Conference Finals. Although James averaged an incredible 35.3 points per game throughout the playoffs, the Cavaliers lost a tough, six-game series to the Orlando Magic. At the conclusion of Game 6, a disgusted James walked off the court without shaking hands with his opponents or speaking with the media. "It's hard for me to congratulate somebody after you just lose to them," he explained later. "I'm a winner. It's not being a poor sport or anything like that. If somebody beats you up, you're not going to congratulate them. That doesn't make sense to me. I'm a competitor." Many basketball analysts, however, dismissed James's words as a poor excuse for unsportsmanlike behavior.

When the 2009-10 NBA season got underway, James continued to make his case for being the best player in the league. He averaged an amazing 29.7 points, 8.6 assists, and 7.3 rebounds per game during the regular season and made the All-Star Team for the sixth straight year. "He's incredible," said NBA Hall of Famer George Gervin. "The combination of speed

The Cavaliers made it to the Eastern Conference playoffs in 2010, but ultimately lost to the Boston Celtics in a crushing defeat that had James ripping off his shirt in frustration at the end of the final game.

and power and athleticism is something you just don't see." In recognition of his performance, James was named NBA Most Valuable Player for the second year in a row. He received 116 out of 123 possible first-place votes from a national panel of sportswriters and broadcasters.

James led the Cavaliers to a 61-21 record and the top seed in the Eastern Conference for the playoffs. Cleveland eliminated the Chicago Bulls in five games in the first round, then moved on to face the Boston Celtics in the conference semifinals. Cleveland fans were excited when the Cavs crushed Boston by 29 points on the road in Game 3 to take a 2-1 series lead. But the Cavs failed to keep the momentum going and lost the next two games in Cleveland. James struggled with a sore elbow that affected his jump shot, and critics claimed that he appeared disinterested at times.

Down 3-2 in the best-of-seven series, however, James turned in an MVP-caliber performance. He posted a triple-double with 27 points, 19 rebounds, and 10 assists. Unfortunately, it was not enough to save the Cavs from elimination. As the final seconds ticked off the clock of the disappointing Game 6 defeat, James ripped off his Cleveland jersey in frustration. "I guess you have to go through a lot of nightmares before you find your dream," he said afterward. Some analysts blamed the Cavs' unexpectedly early playoff exit on the lack of support James received from his teammates. "Anyone with an ounce of basketball knowledge can see the Cavaliers' playoff shortcomings for what they really are," Drew Sharp wrote in the *Detroit Free Press*. "It doesn't matter if you're the greatest player of the day, you're never going to win a best-of-seven playoff series if you're the best player on the floor, but the next three or four best are on the opposing team."

Looking to the Future

By the time James completed his seventh NBA season, he was still only 25 years old. Yet he has already scored more than 15,000 points and posted career averages of 27.8 points, 7.0 rebounds, 7.0 assists, and 1.7 steals per game. To the amazement of many analysts, James seems to keep improving his game with each passing year. He has addressed problems with his shooting mechanics, improved his defensive play, and grown more vocal on the court with his teammates and coaches.

In addition to his outstanding individual contributions, however, James has also shown a remarkable ability to elevate the play of his teammates. His court vision and intelligence enable him to consistently rank among the best playmakers in the league, even though he is also among the top scorers. "When I'm on fire, I can go for a lot of points," he acknowledged. "But getting my teammates involved is good for us in the long run. I can't do it by myself."

James's contract with the Cavaliers was set to expire on July 1, 2010. As that date approached, his future became the subject of intense speculation. Some observers believed that he would remain in Cleveland and try to bring an NBA title to his hometown. The Cavaliers had tried to surround him with talented players during the 2009-10 season—adding Shaquille

O'Neal and Antawn Jamison—in an effort to convince him that the franchise was serious about winning. Following the Cavs' disappointing exit from the playoffs, Cleveland owner Dan Gilbert promised to make whatever other changes were needed to capture an NBA championship.

But many observers believed that James would move on to a new team that plays in a bigger market, such as the New York Knicks, the New Jersey Nets, or the Miami Heat. These teams made roster moves in 2009-10 designed to free up salary room so that they could offer him a blockbuster contract. James insisted that he would choose a team based on where he would have the best chance of winning an NBA title. "The only reason I do what I do on the court is to compete for an NBA championship," he declared. "I understand that, until I win that, I won't go down as one of the greatest players to play this game. Individual accolades definitely come into account, but team is what it's all about. That's my only goal right now."

> "The only reason I do what I do on the court is to compete for an NBA championship," James declared. "I understand that, until I win that, I won't go down as one of the greatest players to play this game. Individual accolades definitely come into account, but team is what it's all about. That's my only goal right now."

Media speculation about his plans became intense in early summer, as sports commentators and fans wondered where James would choose to go. He ultimately announced that he would join the Miami Heat, along with Chris Bosh. The Heat also re-signed Dwyane Wade. Cleveland fans were devastated by the decision, but Miami fans were thrilled and eager to see what the new powerhouse team could accomplish. James made this announcement to fans on his web site: "Next year, I will be playing for the Miami Heat. I would like to thank all of my fans for supporting me and I am looking forward to seeing you guys next season as I chase the NBA Championship."

HOME AND FAMILY

James has two sons with his longtime girlfriend, Savannah Brinson. LeBron James Jr. was born in 2004, and Bryce Maximus James was born in 2007. The family lives in a luxurious home in the suburbs of Akron. "I love [fatherhood] and everything that comes with it," James declared. "The best

*James with his family: his girlfriend, Savannah Brinson, left; his son, LeBron Jr.;
his mother, Gloria James; and his son, Bryce.*

thing is they know who I am. My sons call me Daddy. I see them run around and smile and have fun. They live stress-free." He also remains close to his mother, Gloria, and sports a large tattoo in her honor. "My mother is my everything," he stated. "Always has been. Always will be."

HOBBIES AND OTHER INTERESTS

When he has time to relax, James can often be found playing video games. "I love video games. I'm a video game-aholic," he admitted. "All the guys I grew up with come to the house and every day, all day, we just play video games."

In addition to his remarkable talents on the basketball court, James is well known for the elaborate routines and rituals he performs before every game. During pre-game warm-ups, for instance, he always takes an underhand shot from half court and forms the numbers 3-3-0 with his fingers to symbolize Akron's area code. When James is introduced at the start of a game, he always shakes hands with a lifelong friend at courtside before he runs out onto the floor. Prior to tipoff, he always takes a handful of chalk from a bag near the bench and tosses it into the air before pointing to fans in the upper deck. Finally, he always takes the game ball from the referee and checks it over just before the game begins. "It gets me ready to get out and do what I do best," James explained of his pre-game rituals, "and that's to go out there and play basketball at a high level."

James is also active in volunteer work and community service in the Akron and Cleveland areas. He and his mother started a nonprofit organization called the James Family Foundation to help needy children and support youth programs. The foundation donates 1,000 backpacks full of school supplies each fall and also sponsors an annual fundraiser called the King for Kids Bike-a-thon.

WRITINGS

Shooting Stars, 2009 (with Buzz Bissinger)

HONORS AND AWARDS

Ohio Mr. Basketball (Associated Press): 2001-2003
Gatorade Player of the Year: 2002, 2003
High School Boys Basketball Player of the Year (*Parade Magazine*): 2002, 2003
High School Boys Basketball Player of the Year (*USA Today*): 2002, 2003
McDonald's High School Basketball All-American: 2003
NBA Rookie of the Year: 2004
Olympic Men's Basketball: 2004, bronze medal; 2008, gold medal (with Team USA)
NBA All-Star Team: 2005-2010
NBA All-Star Game Most Valuable Player: 2006, 2008
NBA Most Valuable Player: 2009, 2010

FURTHER READING

Books

Biography Today Sports, Vol. 12, 2004
Christopher, Matt. *On the Court with … LeBron James,* 2008 (juvenile)
Freedman, Lew. *LeBron James: A Biography,* 2008 (juvenile)
Jacobs, L.R. *LeBron James: King of the Court,* 2009 (juvenile)
James, LeBron, and Buzz Bissinger. *Shooting Stars,* 2009
Morgan, David Lee. *The Rise of a Star: LeBron James,* 2003
Savage, Jeff. *Amazing Athletes: LeBron James,* 2005 (juvenile)

Periodicals

Current Biography Yearbook, 2005
Detroit Free Press, May 15, 2010, p.B1
Fortune, Dec. 10, 2007, p.100
New York Times, Feb. 12, 2010, p.B11; Mar. 4, 2010, p.B13
Sporting News, Dec. 20, 2004, p.18
Sports Illustrated, Feb. 18, 2002, p.62; Jan. 13, 2003, p.70; Feb. 25, 2005, p.64;
    Apr. 26, 2006, p.46; June 11, 2007, p.38; Nov. 2007, p.52; Feb. 2, 2009, p.34
Sports Illustrated Kids, Jan. 2004, p.27; Feb. 2005, p.18; June 2008, p.20; Nov.
    2009, p.34
Time, Aug. 4, 2008, p.44
USA Today, Feb. 13, 2008, p.C1; Feb. 11, 2010, p.D5

Online Articles

http://espn.go.com/magazine/vol5no26next.html
    (ESPN The Magazine, "Next: LeBron James," Dec. 10, 2002)
http://www.topics.nytimes.com
    (New York Times, "LeBron James," multiple articles, various dates)
http://www.sportsillustrated.cnn.com/vault/
    (Sports Illustrated, "LeBron James," multiple articles, various dates)

ADDRESS

LeBron James
Cleveland Cavaliers
Gund Arena Company
One Center Court
Cleveland, OH 44115-4001

WORLD WIDE WEB SITES

http://www.lebronjames.com
http://www.nba.com/playerfile/lebron_james
http://www.nba.com/heat
http://www.basketball-reference.com

Taylor Lautner 1992-

American Actor
Star of "The Twilight Saga" Movies

BIRTH

Taylor Lautner was born on February 11, 1992, in Grand
Rapids, Michigan. His father, Dan, is a commercial airline
pilot, while his mother, Deb, is a project manager for a soft-
ware company. The oldest of two children, he has a sister,
Makena, who was born in 1999. He comes from a diverse eth-
nic background. "I'm French, Dutch, and German, and part
Native American," he explained. "My mom has some
Potawatomi and Ottawa Indian in her."

YOUTH

One of Lautner's earliest memories is when his family lost their house and all of their possessions in an electrical fire. He was just four years old. Luckily, his dad was away at work and he and his mom were spending the night at his aunt's house when the blaze broke out. "The police called and told us our house had burned down," recalled Lautner. "If my aunt hadn't invited us to sleep over … well, wow." Afterward, members of his tight-knit community came to the family's aid with donations. "Everyone pulled together for us," he said.

> *When Lautner was just four years old, his house burned down, fortunately when the family was not at home. "The police called and told us our house had burned down. If my aunt hadn't invited us to sleep over … well, wow."*

At age six, Lautner took an interest in martial arts and began studying karate. When he was seven, he traveled to Louisville, Kentucky, to participate in his first karate tournament. While there, he met a Thai-American martial arts coach named Mike Chaturantabut, commonly known as Mike Chat. Chat is the founder of Xtreme Martial Arts—a discipline that blends gymnastics and martial arts—and an actor best known for his role on the television show "Power Rangers: Lightspeed Rescue." Impressed by Lautner's abilities, Chat invited him to attend an Xtreme Martial Arts training camp. Lautner jumped at the chance. "I fell in love," he said. "By the end of the camp, I was doing aerial cartwheels with no hands." He continued to train with Chat for the next several years. By the time he was 12, he had won three junior championships while representing the United States in World Karate Association competitions around the world.

Lautner's self-confidence blossomed as a result of his accomplishments in the martial arts. At age seven, he was encouraged by Chat to audition for a part in a Burger King commercial, but he did not get the job. Nonetheless, he continued to audition for acting roles by periodically flying out to Los Angeles. "I'd go to an audition in the afternoon, take the red-eye back to Grand Rapids, then go to school," he remembered. "I heard 'no, no, no, no' so many times." His luck began to change when, at age 11, he landed a part in a television commercial for the movie *Rugrats* and a role in the 2001 film *Shadow Fury*. At that point his family decided to move to Hollywood. For the next few years, he worked on such TV shows as "The Bernie Mac

Show," "My Wife and Kids," and "Summerland." He also honed his skills as a voiceover artist on animated programs like "What's New, Scooby Doo?" and the TV special "He's a Bully, Charlie Brown."

EDUCATION

Lautner grew up in Hudsonville, Michigan, just outside of Grand Rapids, and attended Jamestown Elementary School. "He was very bright, very well-liked by his peers," recalled Principal Jack DeLeeuw in the *Detroit Free Press*. City of Hudsonville employee Patty Meyer was impressed by his athletic abilities when he walked across the entire stage on his hands during a school show. "He had such talent," Meyer said in the *Detroit Free Press*. "You could see it right away." After the family moved to southern California, Lautner attended Rio Norte Junior High School and Valencia High School. In 2008, due to his busy acting schedule, he began studying privately. He tested out of high school and started taking online college courses.

> **"**
>
> *After the success of* The Adventures of Sharkboy and Lavagirl 3-D, *Lautner began attracting the attention of fans. "Ten-year-old boys were the ones who first recognized me," he said. "I'd be in the store, and boys would whisper to their moms. Then moms would say, 'Excuse me, are you Sharkboy?'"*
>
> **"**

When he lived in Michigan, Lautner studied martial arts at Fabiano's Karate in Holland. Marcus Allen, an instructor who studied with him at the time, remembered that he would "practice for hours and hours." "He was very talented, but he had to work for it, just like everybody else has to," Allen told the *Detroit Free Press*. "He would come in on Sundays for at least four hours to practice." He was also active in baseball, which he started playing at age five, and football, which he took up at age eight.

CAREER HIGHLIGHTS

After moving to California, Lautner continued to audition for roles in TV shows and movies. His break came in 2005 when he nabbed the starring role in *The Adventures of Sharkboy and Lavagirl 3-D*. "Oh, we freaked out," he remembered. "My whole family couldn't sleep for, like, a week." He played Max, a boy who draws the adventures of two superheroes named

Lautner's role as Sharkboy was his first break as an actor.

Sharkboy (who was raised by sharks) and Lavagirl in his journal. One day, after being confronted by a bully, Max finds that he has turned into Sharkboy and that his sister has become Lavagirl. Together, the heroes battle Max's bully as well as a villain named Mr. Electric from the Planet Drool. The movie was a hit with young people, and Lautner began attracting the attention of fans. "Ten-year-old boys were the ones who first recognized me," he said. "I'd be in the store, and boys would whisper to their moms. Then moms would say, 'Excuse me, are you Sharkboy?'"

In addition, Lautner was cast in a supporting role as actor Eugene Levy's son Eliot in the 2005 film *Cheaper by the Dozen 2,* starring comedian Steve Martin. Working with someone as famous as Martin was another turning point for the young actor. "That's when I stopped looking at movie stars as movie stars, and just looked at them as people," he said. In 2008 he played Christian Slater's son on the short-lived TV show "My Own Worst Enemy."

Twilight

Lautner's next big break came when he was up for the role of Jacob Black in the film *Twilight.* The movie was based on the young adult book of the same name by Stephenie Meyer, the first of four books that have become known as "The Twilight Saga." (For more information on Meyer, see *Biography Today,* April 2010.)

When Lautner auditioned for the role of Jacob Black, he was unaware that the books were so popular. Fans of the series, however, were anxiously anticipating the movie version, and he was right at the center of the whirlwind. "Suddenly, it was all over the Internet. I started hearing about all the hype, all the fans. I thought, 'Oh my goodness. If I get this, it'll be huge.' I realized I really want this." Before long, he learned that he got the part. "I was sweating, I was so excited," he confessed.

Twilight is about a teenaged girl named Isabella "Bella" Swan who moves to Forks, Washington, and falls in love with a vampire named Edward Cullen. Bella meets Edward in one of her high school classes and becomes intrigued by his strange ways. When Edward saves her life by stopping an oncoming van with his bare hands, Bella asks her friend Jacob Black about the Cullen family. Jacob, a Quileute Indian, tells her about a local legend concerning vampires who live on animal blood instead of hurting humans. Bella becomes convinced that the Cullens are a family of vampires, and her suspicion proves true when they defend her from a rival vampire clan.

After getting the part of Jacob, Lautner had to become familiar with the books. "I was not a vampire or werewolf fan at all. I'd never even heard

Scenes from "The Twilight Saga": Lautner & Stewart in a scene from New Moon *(top); Lautner in* Twilight *(middle); director Chris Weitz and actors Ashley Greene, Stewart, and Lautner on the set of* New Moon *(bottom).*

of the series," he admitted. "I auditioned for the role, and as soon as I got it, I started reading the books. I'm not a reader, but I really did get hooked on them." In fact, Lautner said, "I actually wasn't much of a book reader at all before the 'Twilight' series. They just draw you in.... They're terrific books." In addition to poring over the novels for character insights, he also studied the cultural background of his character. "Before I went up to Portland [to start filming], I did some research on the Quileute tribe," he said. "I set up a meeting with some real Quileute tribal members in Portland and I got to meet and talk with them. To my surprise, I learned that they are just like me."

Twilight was a huge box office success, and Lautner, along with his co-stars Kristen Stewart (Bella) and Robert Pattinson (Edward), became instant celebrities. He now had to deal with a rapidly growing fan base and intense scrutiny from the media, but he kept it all in perspective. "I don't have time to breathe," he commented at the time. "But it's a lot of fun." At the 2010 People's Choice Awards, *Twilight* won Favorite Movie and Lautner was named Favorite Breakout Movie Actor. His family also became swept up in the *Twilight* enthusiasm. "All of my family lives in Michigan and every family member has read the books, I mean all four of my grandparents, aunts and uncles, everybody! It's just crazy cool that they love it so much!" (For more information on Stewart, see *Biography Today,* Jan. 2010; for more information on Pattinson, see *Biography Today,* Sep. 2009.)

> *"I was not a vampire or werewolf fan at all. I'd never even heard of* ['The Twilight Saga'] *Lautner admitted. "I auditioned for the role, and as soon as I got it, I started reading the books. I'm not a reader, but I really did get hooked on them."*

New Moon

Lautner's character Jacob plays a much larger role in the movie's sequel, *The Twilight Saga: New Moon*, which was released in 2009. In this film, Edward and his family leave Forks out of concern for Bella's safety. Distraught by the loss of Edward, Bella finds herself growing closer to Jacob. She soon learns that he descends from a family of wolves that were transformed into humans by a sorcerer. Jacob vows to protect her against Victoria, a vengeful vampire from a dangerous coven whose threats cause him to shape-shift into a huge werewolf. His transformation leads to a conflict between Edward and Jacob for Bella's affections and escalates the deep-rooted tension between vampires and werewolves in the town of Forks.

The character of Jacob goes through a lot of changes from the first story to the next. So even though Lautner played Jacob in the first film, he still had to prove his ability to tackle the the character's wider physical and emotional range in the sequel. At one point, the producers discussed replacing him because some thought he was too small to play an older version of Jacob. But the fans spoke up on his behalf. According to *Interview* magazine, one fan claimed, "If they don't put him in … there will be a massive *Twilight* fan attack!" Fortunately, *New Moon* director Chris Weitz saw Lautner's potential. "It was a question of letting him hit his range, which included being angry, resentful, dangerous, and violent," Weitz recounted in *People*. In the end, the producers and director of *New Moon* kept him on board.

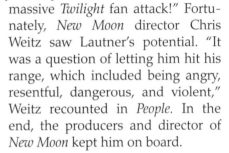

"When I was reading the books, I felt so bad for Jacob," Lautner revealed. "But now that I'm [playing] him, I feel way worse. Bella's toying with Jacob! One moment, she'll want to kiss him, and the next moment, she's ditching him for Edward."

To prepare for the physical demands of playing this chapter in Jacob's life, Lautner had to transform his body. "As soon as I finished filming *Twilight*," he explained, "I got myself a personal trainer, hit the gym five to six days a week, and ate at least 4,000 calories a day." All in all, he gained 30 pounds of muscle for *New Moon*. "At one point, I was going [to the gym] seven days straight. I had put on a lot of weight, and then I started losing it drastically, so I was worried," he stated. "It turned out I was overworking myself. My trainer told me that I couldn't break a sweat, because I was burning more calories than I was putting on." After taking his trainer's advice, he began to notice a difference. "I grew out of a lot of my clothes," he recalled. "I went from a men's small to a men's large."

The love triangle between Edward, Bella, and Jacob is one of the main attractions of the series, and Lautner was sympathetic to his character's situation. "When I was reading the books, I felt so bad for Jacob," he revealed. "But now that I'm [playing] him, I feel way worse. Bella's toying with Jacob! One moment, she'll want to kiss him, and the next moment, she's ditching him for Edward." In addition to portraying the sensitive underdog in the battle for Bella's affection, however, he found that he had to explore

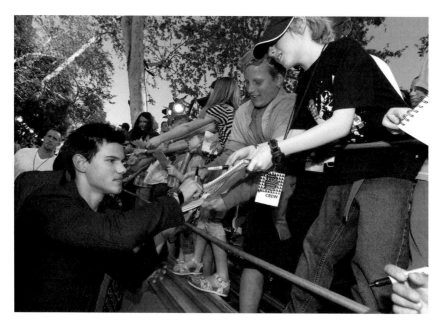

As Lautner's role expanded in New Moon, *he became a fan favorite, as* Twilight *fans pledged allegiance to Team Jacob or Team Edward.*

a complicated personality in the second installment of the series. "There are two sides to Jacob," he explained. "One is like me: friendly, outgoing, and just a nice kid. Then there's the werewolf side, when he's fierce and grumpy." He discovered that playing Jacob in the sequel was almost like playing two roles at the same time: "It's like I'm playing a split personality," he noted. "Which is tricky, because sometimes I've had to play pre- and post-transformation Jacob on the same day of filming."

Earning the Respect of Critics, Co-Stars, and Fans

New Moon was another major hit. Lautner proved himself a commanding screen presence, prompting Karen Levy from *InStyle* magazine to claim that his performance in the movie "makes him a leading man in his own right." His co-stars were likewise impressed with his demeanor on the set. "He's very honest, very open," claimed Kristen Stewart. "It definitely says something about him—he puts people at ease."

Lautner, Stewart, and Pattinson enjoy a close working relationship that Lautner feels has strengthened their on-camera chemistry. "[Jacob and Bella] can tell each other everything. So it was very important for me and Kristen to grow very close," he explained. "[We] can talk things through in rehearsals, and if we're out at dinner, we'll just randomly start talking about the scene we're shooting the next day.... If we weren't able to do those things, I don't know where we'd be." As the young actors continue to work together on the *Twilight* series, Lautner appreciates the positive vibe on set. "We're all really good friends now, so that's really cool," he said.

Lautner has admitted that the attention from *Twilight* fans can become overwhelming. "They are very intense, but it's cool that they're so dedicated and so passionate. They're the reason we're here doing this sequel. So I'm thankful for the fans. But, yeah, they're pretty intense." He has one request of "Team Jacob" supporters: "Please, don't ask me to growl," he begged. "Just wait for the movie." Even though he jokes around with his fans, Lautner remains grateful. "The fans would love anybody who played Jacob," he has insisted. "I'm just lucky to be the one who got the chance."

"There are two sides to Jacob," Lautner explained. "One is like me: friendly, outgoing, and just a nice kid. Then there's the werewolf side, when he's fierce and grumpy." Playing Jacob in the sequel was almost like playing two roles at the same time: "It's like I'm playing a split personality."

Eclipse

In 2010, Lautner and his co-stars filmed the third part of the saga, *The Twilight Saga: Eclipse*. This installment is of personal interest to the actor, who has cited *Eclipse* as his favorite novel in the series. "You have Edward and Jacob teaming up to protect Bella. And then there's the love triangle among all three of them. I think that's the ultimate high point of the series," he said. In this film, Bella awaits high school graduation while grappling with the choice to become a vampire or remain mortal and commit to either Edward or Jacob. This choice is even more difficult because she knows that her decision will impact the course of the war between vampires and werewolves. The Cullens band together with their sworn enemies, the wolf pack, to protect Bella. And in the process, Edward and Jacob become allies as they fight against other vampires.

Reviews of the movie were mixed. Some called it a retread of the previous film, criticizing the dialogue, the acting, and the directing. Other critics praised it as the best film yet in the series, particularly the romantic scenes

Jacob and Bella grow closer in Eclipse, *and Bella faces a difficult choice.*

and the exciting action sequences. Critic Betsy Sharkey offered this praise in the *Los Angeles Times. "The Twilight Saga: Eclipse* is back with all the lethal and loving bite it was meant to have: The kiss of the vampire is cooler, the werewolf is hotter, the battles are bigger, and the choices are, as everyone with a pulse knows by now, life-changing." Reviewer David Germain from *AP* also recognized the film's appeal: "Meyer's millions of fans know what they want in a good *Twilight* movie, and they are going to love *Eclipse*." Indeed, the fans turned out en masse, with the film breaking all box-office records on its release.

Lautner will reprise his role as Jacob in two additional movies based on the final novel in the series, *Breaking Dawn.* Fans were thrilled to learn that this long novel would be made into two movies, rather than condensed into one. In this episode from the saga, Bella is married and pregnant with a unique, supernatural child. The two films adapted from *Breaking Dawn* are scheduled for release in 2011 and 2012.

Balancing His Professional and Personal Life

Although his role in the *Twilight* series made him a star, Lautner has said that his parents have helped him stay levelheaded. "Because of all that's happening for him, we want him to do normal things," Dan Lautner told the *Grand Rapids Press*. "We give him responsibilities at home—chores he has to do. He gets an allotted allowance and he has to budget it. We're trying to teach him things, so that when he goes out on his own, he'll be prepared." His parents often remind him, "You have no idea what's gonna happen tomorrow, so enjoy today. Have fun." Lautner has taken heed of his parents' advice. "It's important to maintain as much normalcy as possible," he said. "Staying true to yourself and spending time with the people you did before, your family and friends. But sometimes it's hard and you definitely have to make adjustments."

> "
>
> *When he's not busy working on a film, Lautner spends his downtime playing football. "It's my indulgence," he admitted. "I've played it my whole life. I always need to have a football in my hand. Like, whenever I'm on set, I'm always holding a ball. If I get a break from shooting, I throw it around with somebody."*
>
> "

Lautner readily admits he is enjoying his success. "I'm having the time of my life," he said. "[The *Twilight*] franchise has allowed me to do what I want to do, meet new people and travel the world." At the same time, he acknowledges the pressures of being a celebrity. When he visited a bookstore near his hometown for the release of *Breaking Dawn* (the final book in the *Twilight* series), he thought he would just put in a brief appearance. Things did not go as planned, however; he ended up signing books for his female fans until 2:00 a.m. "I didn't realize 1,000 girls were gonna be there," he laughed. "I would feel miserable if I left and there were still 100 girls who had been waiting two hours to get my autograph."

Lautner found himself in the public eye once again when he took a supporting role in the 2010 romantic comedy *Valentine's Day*. The movie features a series of interconnected stories about love that all take place on Valentine's Day—some funny, some sad, some poignant, some uplifting. The star-studded cast included Jessica Alba, Jessica Biel, Bradley Cooper, Jamie Foxx, Jennifer Garner, Anne Hathaway, Ashton Kutcher, Queen Latifah, George Lopez, Julia Roberts, and Taylor Swift, among others. "I've only really done one comedy before … and that's why I wanted to be a part of this," Lautner explained. "I wanted to challenge myself to something new, and there's not a better way to do that than with [director] Garry Marshall." Lautner played Willy—the star athlete on the high school track

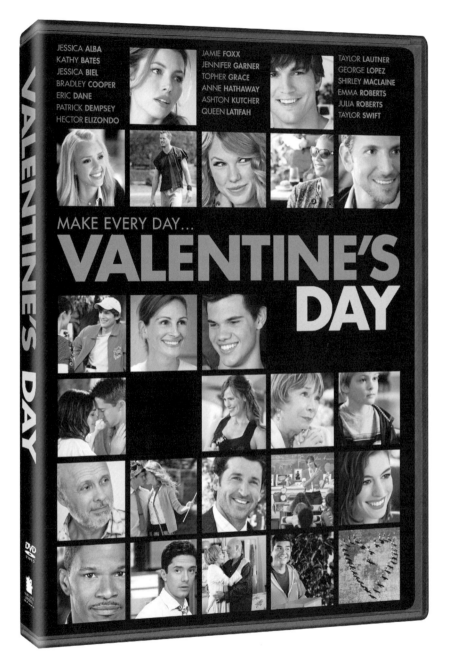

Lautner was part of an all-star cast in the romantic comedy Valentine's Day, *in which he appeared opposite Taylor Swift.*

team—opposite country music sensation Taylor Swift—who played his girlfriend. Their scenes were some of the funniest parts of the movie. Although speculation swirled regarding the pair's brief off-screen romance, Lautner refused to discuss his private life, saying only that Swift is "an amazing girl." When asked what kind of girl he likes to hang out with, he said, "Someone who can be a dork. I don't want anybody too uptight and trying to impress me. If they're outgoing and fun, then that works for me." He also commented, "I'm definitely more for the girl who can smile and laugh all the time and just have a good time!"

HOME AND FAMILY

As his career continues to grow, Lautner remains close to his sister, Makena. "[She] looks up to me, but I also look up to her in a way…. I'm probably going to be one of those brothers who are watching her with boys, which she's probably not going to like too much," he admitted.

Even though he spends most of his time away from his home and family in Michigan, Lautner goes back whenever he has the chance. "I miss the seasons, the green, the lakes. But I miss Hudsonville ice cream the most," he said, referring to the popular brand made in his hometown. "I've looked into getting it shipped to me, but I don't know how they'd do it." He also speaks fondly of the attitude of the people in Michigan, saying that "people are way more down-to-earth."

HOBBIES AND OTHER INTERESTS

When he's not busy working on a film, Lautner spends his downtime playing football. "It's my indulgence," he admitted. "I've played it my whole life. I always need to have a football in my hand. Like, whenever I'm on set, I'm always holding a ball. If I get a break from shooting, I throw it around with somebody." Lautner is a fan of the University of Michigan Wolverines football team and the Detroit Lions, citing Barry Sanders of Detroit Lions fame as one of his all-time favorite players. He is also a hockey fan. In June 2009, he was spotted attending the Stanley Cup finals and rooting for the Detroit Red Wings.

Lautner has confessed to a hearty appreciation of simple food. "I love my steak—no sushi, blue cheese, coconut or beets for me. My trainer actually gets on me, saying, 'You need to start eating chicken; stop eating that red meat!' But I can't help it. I am a steak-and-burger kind of guy." He also loves Mexican and Chinese cuisine.

SELECTED CREDITS

"The Twilight Saga"

Twilight, 2008
The Twilight Saga: New Moon, 2009
The Twilight Saga: Eclipse, 2010

Other Films

The Adventures of Sharkboy and Lavagirl 3-D, 2005
Cheaper by the Dozen 2, 2005
Valentine's Day, 2010

HONORS AND AWARDS

Teen Choice Award: 2009, Choice Movie Fresh Face Male, for *Twilight*
People's Choice Award: 2010 (two awards), Favorite Breakout Movie Actor and Favorite On-Screen Team (with Kristen Stewart and Robert Pattinson), for *Twilight*
Nickelodeon Kids' Choice Award: 2010 (two awards), Favorite Movie Actor and Cutest Couple (with Kristen Stewart), for *The Twilight Saga: New Moon*

FURTHER READING

Books

Leavitt, Amie Jane. *Taylor Lautner,* 2010 (juvenile)
Ryals, Lexi. *Taylor Lautner, Breaking Star: An Unauthorized Biography,* 2009 (juvenile)

Periodicals

Entertainment Weekly, Aug. 21, 2009, p.34; Nov. 20, 2009, p.30; Mar. 12, 2010, p.14; July 2, 2010, p.30
Girl's Life, Dec. 2009, p.42
InStyle, Dec. 2009, p.157
Interview, Aug. 2009, p.62
People, Nov. 30, 2009, p.35
Teen Vogue, Oct. 2009, p.130

Online Articles

http://www.mediablvd.com
(MediaBlvd Magazine, "Taylor Lautner & Edi Gathegi Discuss Their Roles in *Twilight*," Oct. 20, 2008)

http://www.mtv.com
  (MTV, "*Twilight* Actor Taylor Lautner Is Eager To Deliver 'Naked' Line, Master Driving," May 20, 2008)
http://www.people.com/people/taylor_lautner
  (People, "Top 25 Celebs: Taylor Lautner," multiple articles, various dates)
http://www.people.com
  (People, "Taylor Lautner Growing (Literally) with the *Twilight* Franchise," June 1, 2009)
http://www.seattlepi.com
  (Seattle Post-Intelligencer, "Taylor Lautner Talks *New Moon* and *Valentine's Day*," Nov. 19, 2009)
http://movies.yahoo.com
  (Yahoo, "Taylor Lautner," no date)

ADDRESSES

Taylor Lautner
William Morris Agency
One William Morris Place
Beverly Hills, CA 90212

Taylor Lautner
Luber Roklin Entertainment
8530 Wilshire Blvd., 5th Floor
Beverly Hills, CA 90211

WORLD WIDE WEB SITES

http://www.twilightthemovie.com
http://www.stepheniemeyer.com/twilightseries.html

Melinda Merck 1963-

American Forensic Veterinarian
Animal Crime Scene Investigation Expert

BIRTH

Melinda Denise Merck was born on December 22, 1963, in Tucson, Arizona. Her father, Jerry Merck, served in the U.S. Air Force and later worked for IBM. Her mother, Glenda Crowe, was a homemaker when Merck was young. She returned to college to earn a nursing degree when Merck was in high school, and later worked as a nurse. Merck's parents divorced in 1984. She has one younger sister named Melanie.

YOUTH

Merck's family moved around a lot when she was young, depending on where her father was transferred for work. She grew up living in different cities in Texas, Ohio, and Michigan. No matter where she lived, Merck tried to save any injured birds or chipmunks that she found. "I was one of those kids who always had a shoebox with an injured bird or turtle," she recalled. She learned that approach from her grandfather, who lived on a farm and was always taking in stray animals. He was a big influence on her and helped shape her ideas about caring for animals that needed help. By the time she was in kindergarten, Merck already knew that she wanted to become a veterinarian. Then when she was eight years old, she saw a puppy get hit by a car, and this made a big impact on her. She knew that she also wanted to make a difference helping animals and to prevent people from mistreating them.

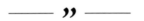

> As a child, Merck tried to save any injured birds or chipmunks that she found. "I was one of those kids who always had a shoebox with an injured bird or turtle," she recalled.

As a young girl, Merck was greatly inspired by the 1966 movie *Born Free*, which told the true story of George and Joy Adamson and their work with lions in Kenya. The story focuses on how the couple came to adopt and raise three lion cubs and how they developed a special attachment to a female cub they named Elsa. When Elsa reached maturity, the Adamsons were determined to help her return to life in the wild, rather than sending her to a zoo. After seeing this movie, Merck said, "I wanted to be Joy Adamson—join the Peace Corps and travel the world saving all the lions and other big cats."

EDUCATION

Merck was a good student who excelled in school. Her favorite subjects were science and biology. She got bored very quickly in her classes and always wanted to learn more, which challenged her teachers to find extra assignments for her. She also loved reading, especially mysteries like the Nancy Drew series. In high school, Merck enjoyed playing team sports like softball, basketball, and volleyball. When she began thinking about college, a high school counselor told her that women didn't become doctors or veterinarians and advised her to choose a different career. But Merck was very stubborn, and that advice only made her more determined to follow her dream.

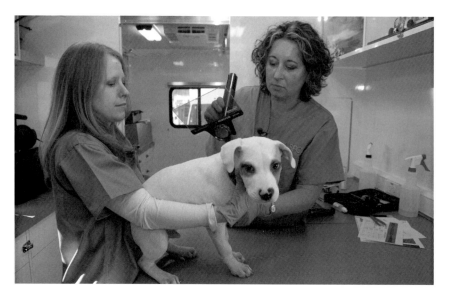

Merck and veterinary assistant Felicia Early doing an examination.

Merck enrolled in the pre-veterinary program at Michigan State University. Although she had graduated at the top of her class in high school, she quickly found that she was unprepared for course work at the college level. She struggled with challenging classes during her first semester, and had to work hard to adjust to college life. By the end of her first year, she had achieved a perfect 4.0 grade point average. In her second year of college, Merck took a test for admission into Michigan State University's school of veterinary medicine. She scored so high on the test that she was offered early admission, a privilege given to only eight students each year.

Merck did well in veterinary school, although the coursework was increasingly difficult. During her second year, she struggled with classes that were exceptionally tough. For the first time in her life, Merck questioned her conviction to become a veterinarian. She transferred to Michigan State University's medical school and began to study radiology. After one semester, however, she realized that she really didn't want to work with people and that she belonged in veterinary school after all. She was allowed to transfer back to the veterinary program and graduated with honors in 1988. She earned her DVM degree, or Doctor of Veterinary Medicine.

CAREER HIGHLIGHTS

In 1990, Merck opened The Cat Clinic, her own veterinary practice in Roswell, Georgia. She explained that her decision to specialize in treating cats was due in part to her childhood love of the movie *Born Free*. But she also felt that cat medicine was a frontier where she could make a difference. Merck felt that cats were the one species that was neglected in veterinary school. At that time, classes were very focused on treating dogs and not much time was given to the study of cats. Diagnosing and treating cats was something of a mystery, and this also interested Merck. "In vet school, cats really got the short end of the stick," she explained. "Dogs are easy to treat. A dog will practically check himself into the hospital and tell you exactly where it hurts. Cats will just curl up and stop eating no matter what's wrong."

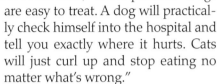

> *Merck felt that cats were neglected in veterinary school: classes focused on treating dogs, and treating cats was considered something of a mystery. "In vet school, cats really got the short end of the stick," she explained. "Dogs are easy to treat. A dog will practically check himself into the hospital and tell you exactly where it hurts. Cats will just curl up and stop eating no matter what's wrong."*

At The Cat Clinic, Merck treated animals regardless of whether their owners could pay for treatment. She was sometimes criticized by people who thought she was crazy to work for free, but Merck had a different opinion. "If I can fix the animal, I'm going to fix the animal. It's the right thing to do," she emphasized. "If you do things for the right reasons, eventually it pays off. It really does. It works. It may take several years to see the benefit, but it pays off. What goes around comes around."

Treating Animal Cruelty Cases

Merck began seeing cases of animal cruelty in her first year of practice. She reported her first case of suspected abuse when a kitten's injuries didn't seem to match its owners' story. "[A] couple brought in a two-pound, eight-week-old Persian kitten that was in a coma with bleeding in the lungs," she reported. "Their reaction was blasé, and their story just didn't add up. So I called the police. The officer had never had a vet report cruelty before. The boyfriend confessed to throwing the kitten against the wall, charges were brought, and the couple fled the state. Being right about that gave me the confidence to pursue other leads." Merck was surprised that no other veterinarians had ever reported suspected abuse to the police. Soon after, she started working with various rescue groups and local animal control agencies.

In 2000, after some particularly bad animal cruelty cases in Atlanta, Georgia, the state passed the Animal Protection Act, making animal cruelty a felony crime (meaning that convictions could result in harsher sentencing than other types of crimes). Merck knew the law would be no good unless people knew how to enforce it. She joined the Georgia Legal Professional for Animals organization and began working to educate people about how to investigate and prosecute animal cruelty cases. Her first task for the organization was to determine how to process a crime scene involving animal cruelty. At that time, Merck could find no information about veterinary forensics, so she turned to experts in human forensics.

Moving into Veterinary Forensics

To learn about forensic techniques and practices, Merck studied human forensics textbooks and worked with local medical examiners and crime scene investigators. She learned how to collect and preserve evidence, such as fluids and fibers, and how to interpret crime scene information, such as bullet trajectories and blood spatter. She then determined how the practices of human forensic investigations could be applied to animal cases. Merck combined the techniques of human forensic science with the specialized knowledge of veterinary medicine. "Forensic veterinary medicine is the application of veterinary medical knowledge to legal matters," she observed. "Evidence associated with any crime has to be analyzed and interpreted in the proper context. In order to properly identify evidence, analyze it, and interpret the findings, you have to know animals and animal behavior. This is what I do and what I bring to a crime scene."

"Forensic veterinary medicine is the application of veterinary medical knowledge to legal matters," Merck observed. *"Evidence associated with any crime has to be analyzed and interpreted in the proper context. In order to properly identify evidence, analyze it, and interpret the findings, you have to know animals and animal behavior. This is what I do and what I bring to a crime scene."*

Merck soon began giving seminars on veterinary forensic investigations for law enforcement and veterinarians. "Veterinarians are naturally the experts on what an animal's response to fear and pain would be," she explained. In her seminars, Merck covered such topics as how to interpret claw marks

Merck with some of her veterinary forensics tools outside of the Mobile Animal CSI unit, part of the ASPCA (American Society for the Prevention of Cruelty to Animals). The tools include an evidence collection kit, an evidence tagging kit, a UV light, an x-ray machine, and a photography kit for identifying evidence at the scene.

at a crime scene and how the marks might indicate a struggle with a perpetrator. She reminded investigators that evidence at a scene would be different: for example, gravesites could be as small as one foot long, not human sized. She pointed out how animal cases differ from human cases, including examples such as animal bleeding patterns, which explained why crime scene photos might lack evidence of the bloody paw prints investigators expected to see.

Within a few years, Merck was spending more time assisting with animal cruelty investigations than she was at her private practice. She helped local law enforcement and animal control officers with crime scene investigations as well as with the examination of live and deceased animal victims. She assisted on cases including animal neglect, hoarding, torture, and dog fighting. Merck traveled the country speaking at veterinary and law enforcement conferences, taught an online course in forensics for veterinarians, and lectured at several university veterinary schools. She spoke on topics related to veterinary forensics and crime scene investigations from a veterinarian's perspective for the Georgia State Bar Association (a professional licensing organization for attorneys). Although it took time away from her private practice, Merck saw tremendous value in the time she spent educating others. "Every time I lecture, whether to vet students, police, or prosecutors both in the U.S. and abroad, there is a ripple effect— they go out and do more for animals."

Finally, in 2006, Merck sold her private practice so that she could devote all of her time to teaching and practicing veterinary forensics. In 2007, she took a full-time position working with the ASPCA (American Society for the Prevention of Cruelty to Animals). In this position, Merck serves as a national and international consultant and expert witness on animal cruelty cases and animal control investigations. It was through the ASPCA that she became involved in one of the most high-profile cases of animal abuse in recent times.

The Michael Vick Dog Fighting Case

In 2007, rising NFL star and Atlanta Falcons quarterback Michael Vick was accused of animal abuse and running a dog fighting ring. Law enforcement authorities were trying to build their case against Vick, but they weren't sure how to prove that he engaged in dog fighting and abuse. They turned to Merck, who conducted a crime scene investigation at property owned by Vick. She located and excavated the graves of many pit bulls and analyzed their remains. In this process, Merck was able to piece together the details of their lives and deaths. Her expert testimony helped put Vick in prison and brought more attention to veterinary forensics as an important tool in law enforcement. "I think the high-profile nature of this case has had a positive impact on animal welfare and cruelty investigations," she observed. "It raised the public's awareness of not only dog fighting but all types of cruelty. It also has had an impact on law enforcement in demonstrating the link between animal cruelty and other types of crimes." Vick was sentenced to 23 months in prison. "It's not about punishment or getting people put into jail," Merck argued. "It's about protecting the animals. If we're not the voice for that animal, who is?"

During this time, Merck also compiled her knowledge and experience processing crime scenes in the book *Veterinary Forensics: Animal Cruelty Investigations*, published in 2007. The book was well received and widely praised. The Veterinary Information Network recommended it as "a book that should be in every clinic." A reviewer for *Veterinary Pathology* said the book "helps fill the void in the forensic veterinary medical literature. Nobody could argue with Dr. Merck's enthusiasm and zeal to make us aware of an important topic that we would prefer to ignore, but should not." *Midwest Book Review* praised the book as a "resource essential for

Merck excavating a grave site during an animal cruelty investigation.

animal cruelty investigators." Merck also co-wrote a second book, *Veterinary Forensic Investigation of Animal Cruelty: A Guide for Veterinarians and Law Enforcement*.

In 2008, Merck helped found the International Veterinary Forensic Sciences Association. This professional organization works to continue developing veterinary forensics and educate the animal welfare community, law enforcement agencies, courts, and veterinarians on the importance of veterinary forensics. Merck was honored in 2009 with the U.S. Department of Justice Outstanding Investigation or Case Award for her work on the Michael Vick trial. It was the first time that an animal-related case had received such an award.

Around this time Merck also helped design and launch the nation's first formal veterinary forensic sciences program at the University of Florida. As part of the veterinary master's degree program, the veterinary forensics certificate gives veterinarians the training to recognize crime against animals and the tools to do something about it. She explained the need for the program by saying, "A problem is that once [a vet] becomes suspicious, they may not have been taught what to do next." Merck currently teaches at the University of Florida while continuing to investigate cases for the ASPCA.

Handling Difficult Cases

During her investigations, Merck has seen horrific cases of animal torture, neglect, and other forms of abuse. She is often asked how she can work in a field that requires her to closely examine and document the details of such cases. "It is certainly difficult to work with these cases because they represent the ultimate breakdown of the human-animal bond," she acknowledged. "I think my work as a veterinarian has helped me because you learn to compartmentalize in order to do your job—you cannot succumb to emotion while working on an animal or case. For cruelty, I turn it into a puzzle that I have to solve. My goal is to gather evidence to find and successfully prosecute the offender. I realize that what's done is done and I have to work toward justice. It is very hard because of my empathy for animals, but the best thing I can do for them is be their voice."

Merck channels her feelings about a case into positive action, focusing on being objective and seeking justice for the animal victims. She works hard to try to determine what really happened to them, gathering evidence and bringing it into a legal case that can be prosecuted. It also helps Merck to remember that she works as part of a team, and that the entire outcome of each case does not rest completely on her shoulders. She believes that people with special skills or knowledge have an obligation to use those talents for the benefit of society. In this way, she puts her work into perspective. "In every case we make a difference. Even if the animal has died, we can prevent it from happening again."

> "
>
> *"It's not about punishment or getting people put into jail,"* Merck said about investigating and prosecuting animal cruelty cases. *"It's about protecting the animals. If we're not the voice for that animal, who is?"*
>
> "

Merck also recognizes the importance of her own recuperation time after a particularly difficult case. She makes sure to spend time between cases with her own pets. She recharges and relaxes by reading and watching television. She also finds it particularly rewarding to see how well the animals she has rescued are doing in their new homes. Merck is committed to placing animals rescued during cruelty cases into foster homes, special rehabilitation shelters, or permanent homes.

Despite the emotional strain of some cases, Merck has said that the part of her work that she enjoys most is investigating animal cruelty. "It is challenging to figure out these puzzles, each case is different. And working with the investigators and prosecutors is always interesting. The casework is satisfying because I am giving the animal a voice," she commented. "The best part of the job is when we succeed—this can mean a conviction, successful intervention or when the animal is now protected from future harm. I work with a group of investigators and prosecutors who support going after the criminals who commit cruelty—that continually validates what I am doing and keeps me motivated."

HOME AND FAMILY

Merck lives in Gainesville, Florida, with an ever-changing assortment of dogs and cats, nearly all rescued from bad situations.

HONORS AND AWARDS

Outstanding Investigation or Case Award (U.S. Department of Justice): 2009, for her work in the investigation of the Michael Vick case

FURTHER READING

Periodicals

Atlanta Journal-Constitution, Mar. 17, 2005, p.JF2
Kansas City (MO) Star, Aug. 5, 2009
People, Mar. 26, 2007, p.113
St. Petersburg Times, June 28, 2009, p.E1
USA Today, Oct. 9, 2007

Online Articles

http://veterinarynews.dvm360.com/dvm/article/articleDetail.jsp?id=622205
    (dvm360, "The New Welfare War," Sep. 1, 2009)
http://veterinarynews.dvm360.com/dvm/article/articleDetail.jsp?id=501366
    (dvm360, "Reporting Suspected Animal Abuse Getting Easier, Experts Say," Mar. 1, 2008)
http://veterinarymedicine.dvm360.com/vetmed/Medicine/ArticleStandard
    /Article/detail/491398
    (dvm360, "The Veterinary Medicine Interview: Dr. Melinda D. Merck," Feb. 1, 2008)
http://www.veterinarypracticenews.com/vet-industry-people/profiles-in
    -medicine/voice-for-justice.aspx
    (Veterinary Practice News, "Voice for Justice: Melinda Merck, DVM," Oct. 2009)

ADDRESS

Melinda Merck, DVM
ASPCA
424 East 92nd Street
New York, NY 10128

WORLD WIDE WEB SITE

http://www.veterinaryforensics.com
http://www.aspca.org

Orianthi 1985-

Australian Singer and Guitarist
Guitarist for Michael Jackson and Singer of
"According to You"

BIRTH

Orianthi Panagaris, known professionally as Orianthi, was born on January 22, 1985, in Adelaide, the largest city in South Australia. Her unusual first name came from her Greek grandmother and is pronounced "Or-ee-AN-thee." She was the first child of Peter Panagaris, a musician, and his wife Susanne; they had a second daughter, Tina, 11 months after Orianthi was born.

YOUTH

With a father in the business, Orianthi grew up surrounded by a wide variety of music. Through her father's extensive collection of records, she heard classic rock from the 1960s and 1970s, which featured such guitarists as Jimi Hendrix, Eric Clapton, and Carlos Santana. At the same time, she listened to hard rock guitar bands like Van Halen and Def Leppard on the radio.

Orianthi also started playing music at a young age. Her father kept plenty of instruments around the house, and she started playing piano when she was only three. At six she picked up her first guitar, an acoustic model that she learned to play in classical style. She began playing the guitar all the time, at home and at school. At age 10 she was playing guitar in the pit orchestra for an Adelaide University Theatre production of the musical "Oklahoma."

Orianthi was 11 when her life changed after hearing Carlos Santana in concert. The Mexican-American guitarist had produced the hit singles "Black Magic Woman" and "Oye Como Va" with his group Santana in the early 1970s and was known for the blistering guitar solos that highlighted his band's Latin-flavored rock. After the show, "I begged my dad to get me a second-hand electric guitar so I could be like Carlos, and that was it, no more acoustic," she remembered. "After that, I would buy all of Carlos's videos—on VHS!—which I kept rewinding to try and learn his solos. I totally wore out the tapes."

> **After Orianthi saw Carlos Santana performing live for the first time, "I begged my dad to get me a second-hand electric guitar so I could be like Carlos, and that was it, no more acoustic," she remembered. "After that, I would buy all of Carlos's videos—on VHS!—which I kept rewinding to try and learn his solos. I totally wore out the tapes."**

Orianthi worked hard to perfect her guitar skills, practicing as much as five or six hours a day. As a teenager she played with two cover bands that performed popular Top 40 songs in pubs, clubs, and talent shows. Her father helped her record a demo CD, *Under the Influence,* on which she paid tribute to the great guitarists who had inspired her. She mailed the CD with a letter to guitar companies, music magazines, and music managers all over the world. She was only 14 years old, but her hard work eventually paid off with her first management deal.

Orianthi recorded her first CD at age 14 and has been playing professionally ever since.

EDUCATION

Growing up in Adelaide, Orianthi attended several schools, where her focus on the guitar sometimes made her the target of bullies. "I was called a freak because I was so engrossed in music," she noted. At lunchtime at school, if she'd left her guitar at home, she would make one from a milk carton and some rubber bands. She changed primary school at least five times, once so she could play soccer, another favorite activity. She finally ended up at Cabra Dominican College, a private high school in Adelaide, where she found friends who supported her. Nevertheless, by age 15 she was missing so many classes because of her music that she started home schooling instead. She continued with this distance learning program for another year before leaving to concentrate on music. "It was so hard to keep focused on history and math when all I wanted was to be a guitarist," she said.

CAREER HIGHLIGHTS

Pursuing Her Musical Dreams

Orianthi spent most of her teenage years developing her musical talents, and the hard work paid off with some impressive gigs supporting international artists during their Australian tours. At age 15 she opened for one of her idols, Grammy-winning guitarist Steve Vai, who got his start working with rock icons like Frank Zappa, David Lee Roth, and the band Whitesnake. At age 16 she played as the opening act for ZZ Top, the noted blues-rock trio and members of the Rock and Roll Hall of Fame. At the same time she continued playing with cover bands. She loved guitar so much that "I would put guitar solos in the songs, even though they weren't there." But she also began working with a vocal coach so she could sing with the group. At first she was shy about singing, "but as we rehearsed more I became more comfortable with it," she said. "I think once you start singing, you can connect with more people." By age 18 she was fronting her own band, DropD, singing and playing guitar at clubs around Adelaide.

That same year Carlos Santana played another important role in the aspiring rocker's musical development. He had returned to Australia for another tour, but this time Orianthi didn't watch from the audience. Santana had heard her demo CD and invited her to his pre-concert sound check in Adelaide. "We wound up jamming, and then he invited me to join him onstage that night," she recalled. She ended up playing for 45 minutes in front of 15,000 fans, even getting her own solo. "It was nerve-wracking but once I was up there it was fantastic," she said. Even more important, Santana took a video of the concert back to his guitar manufacturer, Paul Reed Smith Guitars. In 2004 PRS Guitars invited her to Los Angeles to play at NAMM, one of the world's largest music product trade shows. Eventually PRS Guitars became her sponsor, providing her with guitars and contacts in the music industry.

> **"**
>
> *After Santana listened to her demo CD, he invited Orianthi to his sound check. "We wound up jamming, and then he invited me to join him onstage that night," she recalled. She ended up playing for 45 minutes in front of 15,000 fans, even getting her own solo. "It was nerve-wracking but once I was up there it was fantastic," she said.*
>
> **"**

Orianthi kept playing at trade shows around the world and increasing her exposure. While bystanders may have wondered whether she earned stage time because of her good looks, music insiders knew better. In 2005, her idol Carlos Santana was interviewed on Australian television about her skill. "It's not cute any more. It's seriously [awesome]," he said. "If I was going to pass the baton to somebody, she would be my first choice." While playing at another NAMM show she met record executives at Geffen, who signed her to an international recording contract in late 2006.

Orianthi began working on her first full-length CD, *Violet Journey*, which she released in 2007. On this collection of original material, she wrote the songs, sang, played guitar, and also played almost all of the other instruments, including bass, drums, and percussion. She also produced the entire album, engineering and mixing the tracks herself. *Violet Journey* was distributed by a minor label and didn't make much of a splash.

Still, Orianthi kept working to advance her career. She wrote and performed the song "Now or Never" for the 2007 movie *Bratz,* a film targeting the young girls she hoped to inspire with her music. That same year she worked with two great guitarists: she served as the opening act for Steve Vai's international tour and she was invited to participate in Eric Clapton's Crossroads Guitar Festival in 2007. Clapton is the legendary guitarist who is the only person to have been inducted into the Rock and Roll Hall of Fame three times: with the groups Cream and the Yardbirds, and as a solo artist. He founded the Crossroads Festival, which features some of the world's greatest guitar players in concert, to benefit the Crossroads addiction rehab center. At the 2007 festival in Chicago, Orianthi played some of her own songs on stage and also had the chance to meet some of her guitar idols, including Clapton and blues legend B. B. King.

Working with Michael Jackson

In 2009 Orianthi started getting worldwide attention for her talents. It began in February, when she was invited to perform at the Grammy Awards with country superstar Carrie Underwood. "I was so nervous, looking out into the audience and seeing people like [U2's singer] Bono and Paul McCartney!" she noted. Nevertheless, her blistering solo on Underwood's "Last Name" brought her lots of attention. When someone saw the video of her performance and contacted her via MySpace to audition for singer Michael Jackson's upcoming tour, she thought it was a joke. The audition was real, however, and soon she was performing the guitar solo in "Beat It" for the superstar. "He started walking me up and down the stage," she remembered. "And he asked, 'Can you play that solo for me when walking at this pace?' And I said, 'Totally.' It was an amazing moment." She was soon signed for Jackson's tour, which was scheduled to play 50 concerts at the O2 Arena in London, England.

The tour was to launch a comeback for Jackson, whose 1982 album *Thriller* was the biggest selling record of all time. Orianthi and a huge cast of

Orianthi worked with Michael Jackson preparing for a series of comeback concerts in London in 2009. Jackson died suddenly before the concerts took place, but the rehearsals, which were filmed and produced in the film This Is It, *prominently featured Orianthi's guitar work.*

singers, musicians, and dancers rehearsed with Jackson six days a week for three months. "Rehearsals were intense," she noted. "[Jackson] was really particular. He wanted to be sure everything was perfect for his fans." She found herself learning not just about showmanship, but more about playing rhythm guitar in a group. "Going into it, I thought it would be all about playing guitar solos," she noted. "But the majority of it was playing chords and funky rhythms." The rehearsals were thrilling and intensive, but Jackson seemed up to the challenge. Orianthi was stunned when he suffered a heart attack and died in June 2009, less than three weeks before the tour was due to begin. Instead of performing in concert with Jackson, she sang and played at his memorial tribute, which was televised to millions of viewers around the world. "I wish he was still around," she shared. "He made me believe in myself more, and I learned so much."

The outpouring of public grief at Jackson's death, as well as curiosity about his final tour, led to a film that documented the show's rehearsals. *This Is It* was released in October 2009, and Orianthi's rocking guitar solos were featured prominently. The film showed "the whole process of putting together what would have been the biggest show on Earth," she revealed. "You can just see how excited he was about it. It was his vision." Although the film was only in theaters a few weeks, it earned $260 million worldwide and introduced Orianthi to a wider audience.

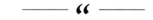

When Orianthi auditioned for Michael Jackson, she performed the guitar solo in "Beat It." "He started walking me up and down the stage," she remembered. "And he asked, 'Can you play that solo for me when walking at this pace?' And I said, 'Totally.' It was an amazing moment."

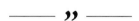

Becoming an All-Star Musician

Orianthi's record company capitalized on the publicity by moving up the release of her first major-label album, *Believe,* to October 2009. She co-wrote eight of the album's 11 tracks, all of which included a guitar solo. "It's bringing the '80s back, in a way. I just love that music," she said of the album. "I hope [listeners] want to put it in their car and not want to change it." Many critics observed that the artist achieved a power pop feel to the recording, and compared her to artists like Avril Lavigne, Kelly Clarkson, and the group Paramore. In *Billboard,* Lars Brandle called *Believe*

Orianthi's fame has grown as she has appeared with different musicians. In 2010 she made several appearances on "American Idol," including this collaboration with Mary J. Blige.

"essentially a conventional pop album with an utterly unconventional guitar solo on each track." Its first single, "According to You," hit the top 20 of *Billboard*'s Hot 100 chart and peaked at No. 4 on the pop chart. To prove she hadn't lost any of her rock edge, she also released a video for the instrumental number "Highly Strung," which she wrote and recorded with Steve Vai. Both tunes received a lot of attention, and the album itself hit No. 1 on the *Billboard* New Artist and Heatseekers charts.

Through late 2009 and early 2010, Orianthi kept building momentum with several appearances on television. Besides several talk shows, she also played at an NFL game in Miami in December 2009 and performed her single "According to You" live on "American Idol" in 2010. She became part of two all-star recordings, contributing guitar and backing vocals to the 2010 remake of "We Are the World," which benefited victims of the Haiti earthquake. She and Steve Vai contributed guitar solos to R&B diva Mary J. Blige's version of the Led Zeppelin classic "Stairway to Heaven," and the all-star group performed the song live on the "American Idol Gives Back" special. Throughout the spring and summer of 2010 she appeared as a supporting act for Daughtry, John Mayer, Adam Lambert, and Kid Rock. "I don't consider these opportunities stepping stones, I consider them honors," she said of these chances to play with music stars.

> *As a female rock guitarist, Orianthi has often encountered skepticism when playing her guitar on stage. "It's like you have to prove yourself to them. Hopefully, I can change that a little bit so more guys can look at women playing the guitar and take them seriously. Anyone can do anything if they really have a passion for it."*

Although the life of a rock star is full of potential pitfalls, Orianthi plans to focus on the music, not the lifestyle. "It's a crazy industry," she commented. "I'm not into the partying, I'm a pretty healthy person. I don't like drinking or doing drugs but it does happen and I hear it's insane. But once you go off the rails like that, you can't really take the craft that seriously—that becomes your life. I've seen young musicians and actresses go down that self-destructive path. I'll probably overdose on spinach before any of that." Her future career plans include more pop-rock music and an all-instrumental album, as well as further partnerships with other musicians and singers. "I love fronting my own band and singing and playing my own material," she said, but she stressed that "I also love collaborating and just being the guitar player. I get the same rush from doing both."

Orianthi also wants to inspire her listeners to share her love of music and playing. In 2010 Paul Reed Smith Guitars brought out the Orianthi signature model, a relatively affordable electric guitar which she hoped would bring more girls to the field. "Being a female guitar player is not easy. It's kind of like being a male ballerina," she said, drawing a parallel to another gender stereotype. "It's a guy thing. And I accept that. But I love it as much as they love it." Early in her career, she often encountered skepticism when playing her guitar on stage. "It's like you have to prove yourself to them. Hopefully, I can change that a little bit so more guys can look at women playing the guitar and take them seriously. Anyone can do anything if they really have a passion for it." Her attitude is to ignore the naysayers and concentrate on making the best music she can. "My outlook on life is to keep looking up," she remarked. "If you're looking down, you don't see the light. For me, it's all about embracing that and thinking positively."

HOME AND FAMILY

Orianthi moved from Australia to Los Angeles in 2006 to pursue her dream of a musical career. The musician, who is single, said she has adjusted to living in a new country, although she misses her family and all the animals on their suburban Adelaide home. She often has her sister Tina for company, both in Los Angeles and on the road. She also has two small dogs, Pumba and Harriett.

FAVORITE MUSIC

Although Orianthi loves all kinds of music, including pop and country, she considers rock and blues guitarists her most important influences. She has been lucky to play with her two idols, Carlos Santana and Steve Vai, and cites several others as favorites. These include British rocker Eric Clapton, American blues man B. B. King ("he can hit one note and move you"), and the late American blues rocker Stevie Ray Vaughan, who "played with such fire [and] attitude." She also once played with the funk-rock singer and guitarist Prince, who called her up and invited her to jam with his band after seeing videos of her performances.

HOBBIES AND OTHER INTERESTS

When she isn't on the road, the mostly vegetarian Orianthi loves cooking and baking for her family and friends. When she's touring she relaxes by watching TV, walking, and going to the gym. She also has a very strong love for animals; she grew up with the usual cats and dogs, but also had rabbits, pigeons, doves, mice, and fish at various times during her childhood. Some of her favorite pets were ducks; at one point her family had seven of them on their property.

CREDITS

Violet Journey, 2007
"Now or Never," on *Bratz,* 2007 (movie soundtrack)
Believe, 2009
This Is It, 2009 (movie)

FURTHER READING

Periodicals

The Age (Melbourne, Australia), July 7, 2007
Billboard, Nov. 7, 2009, p.27; Jan. 30, 2010, p.35
Boston Herald, Oct. 26, 2009, p.E3
Entertainment Weekly, Oct. 16, 2009, p.58; Oct. 30, 2009, p.58
Guitar Edge Magazine, Nov. 23, 2009; Jan. 24, 2010
Houston Chronicle, Oct. 28, 2009, p.1
Los Angeles Times, Oct. 30, 2009
Sunday Mail (Adelaide, Australia), Oct. 11, 2009, p.15; Feb. 28, 2010, p.4
USA Today, Oct. 26, 2009, p.2D

Online Articles

http://www.mtv.com
  (MTV, "Michael Jackson Guitarist Orianthi Is 'Bringing the '80s Back' with Debut," Oct. 26, 2009)
http://www.musicsa.com.au
  (Music SA, "Orianthi Autobiography," 2006)
http://www.prsguitars.com
  (Paul Reed Smith Guitars, "Orianthi," Feb. 26, 2010)
http://www.rollingstone.com
  (Rolling Stone, "Breaking: Orianthi," Dec. 16, 2009)
http://www.teenmusic.com
  (Teen Music, "Exclusive Interview! At the Hard Rock with Orianthi!," Feb. 6, 2009)
http://www.truthinshredding.com
  (Truth in Shredding, "Orianthi: Truth in Shredding Exclusive Interview," Nov. 12, 2009)

ADDRESS

Orianthi
Interscope Geffen A&M Records
2220 Colorado Avenue
Santa Monica, CA 90404

Orianthi
19 Entertainment
8560 West Sunset Blvd.
West Hollywood, CA 90069

WORLD WIDE WEB SITE

http://www.orianthi.com

Zoë Saldana 1978-
American Actress
Star of the Hit Movies *Avatar* and *Star Trek*

BIRTH

Zoë Yadira Zaldaña Nazario was born on June 19, 1978, in New Jersey. Her father was from the Dominican Republic, and her mother was from Puerto Rico. Saldana has two sisters, Mariel and Cisely, one older and one younger. She also has one step-brother. Saldana changed the spelling of her last name when she started acting, to make it easy for people to pronounce. "I wanted to make it easier for everyone," she claimed. "Zaldaña is too complicated for everyone else. I would love to have kept my original name."

YOUTH AND EDUCATION

Saldana grew up in the Queens borough of New York. When she was 10 years old, her father died in a car accident. "My parents were a good team at raising us, they were very good friends, and my mom never expected to have to raise us without my father," she recalled. "It was a shock for all of us, for my mom having to become the father and the mother, and we did lose a lot of innocence and have to mature quickly." After her father's death, her mother sent Saldana and her sisters to live with relatives in the Dominican Republic. She lived there from about the age of 10 to 17. While there, she studied dance at the Espacio de Danza Dance Academy. There she learned ballet as well as other forms of dance and dreamed of becoming a ballerina.

> "My parents were a good team at raising us, they were very good friends, and my mom never expected to have to raise us without my father," Saldana said about her father's death. "It was a shock for all of us, for my mom having to become the father and the mother, and we did lose a lot of innocence and have to mature quickly."

When she was 17 years old, Saldana and her sisters moved back to New York to live with their mother. Saldana loved dancing, but she also developed a new interest in theater. She began performing with the Faces theater group, which put on improvised plays with positive messages for teens. Faces performed in schools and community centers and dealt with such real-life issues as substance abuse, violence, suicide, and HIV/AIDS. Faces gave Saldana valuable acting experience, and she also enjoyed helping young people deal with important issues. Around the same time, she was also performing with the New York Youth Theater, where she appeared in a production of the musical *Joseph and the Amazing Technicolor Dream Coat*. Her performance caught the attention of a talent scout, and Saldana was recruited by a talent agency. This helped her land her first movie role.

CAREER HIGHLIGHTS

Saldana made her movie debut in the role of Eva Rodriguez in the 2000 movie *Center Stage*. This movie followed the progress of a group of young

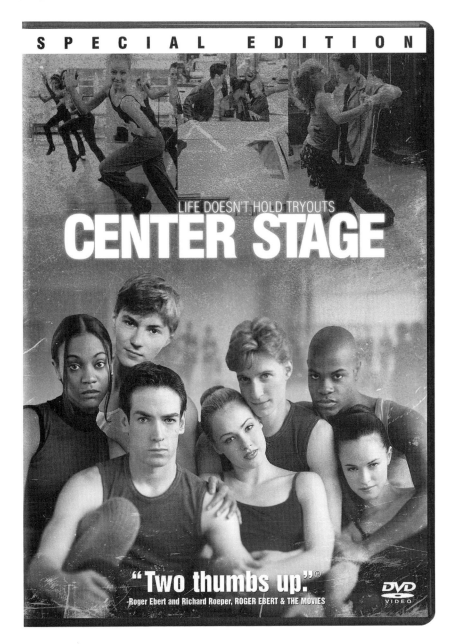

Drawing on her dance training, Saldana played a young gifted ballet dancer in Center Stage.

ballet dancers enrolled in the fictional American Ballet Academy. Saldana's dance background helped her land the role, in which she played a rebellious young woman who must learn to take dancing more seriously if she wants to succeed. For Saldana, the role was bittersweet, because she had already decided to leave dancing behind in order to pursue an acting career. The movie received lukewarm reviews, with most critics acknowledging that it was clearly a movie made for teen audiences. However, *Center Stage* gathered fans among younger viewers who enjoyed the movie for its coming-of-age story and its view into the drama of a competitive ballet school.

Center Stage led to more roles in teen movies. Saldana had a minor part in the 2001 musical romantic comedy *Get Over It,* a story about a high school jock who gets dumped by his girlfriend and then tries to win her back by signing up for the school play, the Shakespeare comedy *A Midsummer Night's Dream.* She went on to win a co-starring role alongside Britney Spears in the 2002 movie *Crossroads.* This movie tells the story of three childhood friends who decide to travel from their small Georgia hometown to Los Angeles, where one of the three has an audition for a record contract. Neither of these movies was commercially successful, although *Crossroads* became popular mainly among Spears's fans. In these roles, Saldana gained more acting experience and was offered more movie parts as a result.

In the 2002 movie *Drumline,* Saldana played the role of Laila, a college cheerleader who develops a romantic relationship with the movie's star, played by Nick Cannon. *Drumline* tells the story of a talented but untrained young drummer who is recruited to join the ranks of a prestigious Southern university marching band. As the story unfolds, tension grows between the young newcomer and the drum section leader as the band prepares for an important national competition. *Drumline* did not do particularly well in theaters, but the movie found an enthusiastic audience among young viewers who were drawn in by the story and the performance scenes with the marching band drum section. Saldana and Cannon shared a nomination for that year's MTV Movie Award for best kiss in a love scene.

Transitioning from Teen Roles

Saldana successfully moved away from teen movies with her appearance in *Pirates of the Caribbean: The Curse of the Black Pearl,* released in 2003. She played Anamaria, the lone female pirate who casts a spell on Captain Jack Sparrow. Though her role was small, she was credited with creating one of the movie's best comic scenes with Johnny Depp.

In 2004, Saldana appeared in *The Terminal*, a movie starring Tom Hanks as Viktor Navorski, an Eastern European tourist stranded in New York City's JFK airport. While Navorski is in flight, the government of his home country is overthrown and the U.S. refuses to recognize the new government. He can't enter the U.S. because his passport is viewed as invalid, but he also can't return home because all flights in and out of his home country have been suspended. Stuck between two countries, he is forced to take up residence in the airport terminal. The story unfolds as Navorski tries to get home, making friends with various airport employees and building a life for himself in the terminal in the meantime. Saldana plays Dolores Torres, an immigration agent working in the terminal where Navorski is stranded. Her performance earned her a Young Hollywood One to Watch Award from *Movieline* magazine.

> **"**
>
> *"I don't feel that there are enough roles that resemble the American women nowadays in Hollywood,"* Saldana argued. *"It's almost an insult when you read scripts and you see that the guy's the hero."*
>
> **"**

In 2005, Saldana starred in *Guess Who?*, a romantic comedy remake of the 1967 critically acclaimed drama *Guess Who's Coming to Dinner*. In the remake, Saldana played a young black woman who brings her white fiancé, played by Ashton Kutcher, home to meet her family, much to the distress of her father, played by Bernie Mac. Although *Guess Who?* was not very successful either with critics or at the box office, Saldana earned praise for her performance. She was nominated for best actress at the NAACP Image Awards, the Black Movie Awards, and the Black Reel Awards.

Star Trek

Saldana's breakout role was in the highly anticipated 2009 *Star Trek* movie, in which she played communications specialist Uhura. This movie is a prequel to the groundbreaking original 1966 "Star Trek" television show, which began a science fiction storytelling legacy that has grown to include five additional TV series, 10 other movies, and countless books. Many of these productions featured the same characters at different points in their lives, building a long continuing story that developed over more than 30 years. In the 2009 *Star Trek* movie, new actors were cast to portray the same characters shown in the original 1966 series, but in an earlier time period when they were young Starfleet Academy students being trained as spaceship crew

Saldana as Uhura, right, with fellow Star Trek *cast members Anton Yelchin (Chekov), Chris Pine (James T. Kirk), an unnamed cast member, Karl Urban (Dr. Leonard "Bones" McCoy), and John Cho (Sulu). Not shown: Zachary Quinto as Spock.*

members. In this movie, an emergency finds the group of young cadets suddenly assigned as crew members on the new starship *Enterprise*. A complicated and adventure-filled story unfolds, involving personality conflicts, space battles, an evil enemy determined to destroy Earth and the planet Vulcan, time travel, and a series of events that change the future for everyone.

Before making the movie, Saldana had only seen a couple of episodes of the original "Star Trek" TV series. She was excited to take on the role, however. "I'm very proud to say I am a geek," she boasted. "But I'm kind of a cool geek. I grew up in a very sci-fi home so I've seen a lot of sci-fi movies, from *Dune* to *Alien, 2001, ET, Batteries Not Included....* All these films I go crazy for. But never *Star Trek*." Among the episodes of the original series that Saldana did watch was a pivotal one in which William Shatner as Captain James T. Kirk and Nichelle Nichols as Uhura share a kiss. This episode made history as the first interracial kiss shown on TV.

Saldana's limited exposure to the "Star Trek" TV series and subsequent movies was intentional. After she got the part, she listened to advice from director J.J. Abrams. "I followed J.J.'s advice. He said, 'If I have to advise you guys at all, I would advise you not to watch [the original TV series]. Just inform yourself of the whole concept of 'Star Trek,' if you're not already a Trekkie or fan. I don't want you to cloud whatever contribution you guys can make yourselves to the role that you are jumping into.' I thought that was very encouraging." However, Saldana did meet with Nichelle Nichols to discuss the role and character of Uhura.

Star Trek received mixed reviews. Some critics and fans viewed the movie as a re-invention of the well-known *Star Trek* world and welcomed the new cast of young actors as a fresh approach to the series. But some were angry that so many changes were made to the basic *Star Trek* premise and complained that the movie swept away 30-plus years of *Star Trek* history in order to make a new beginning. Saldana's performance was widely praised, however. The *National Review* said that "Saldana smolders as a young Uhura," while *Entertainment Weekly* said "Saldana gives Uhura a sultry spark." According to *Daily Variety*, "Saldana is vibrant as the female crew member who bestows her favors on one officer to the exasperation of another."

Avatar

Saldana's next big screen role was in the 2009 blockbuster hit movie *Avatar*. In this 3D science fiction / fantasy movie, she played Neytiri, an entirely computer-generated character. The story of *Avatar* takes place in the year 2154, on the alien world of Pandora, a jungle-covered planet located in the Alpha Centauri system many light years from Earth. As the story begins, the audience learns that human negotiations with Na'vi natives of Pandora have turned violent. A corporate group is mining a rare mineral on Pandora that is needed to solve Earth's energy crisis. A former U.S. Marine named Jake is recruited

——— " ———

"I'm very proud to say I am a geek," Saldana boasted. *"But I'm kind of a cool geek. I grew up in a very sci-fi home so I've seen a lot of sci-fi movies, from* **Dune** *to* **Alien, 2001, ET, Batteries Not Included**.... *All these films I go crazy for. But never* **Star Trek."**

——— " ———

to travel to the human outpost on Pandora and infiltrate the Na'vi, with the goal of removing obstacles to the mining operation. Humans cannot breathe in Pandora's atmosphere, but the Avatar Program allows human "drivers" to have their consciousness linked to a remotely controlled biological body that can survive in the toxic air. These avatar bodies are genetically engineered hybrids that combine human and Na'vi DNA.

As Jake, in avatar form, is finding his way on Pandora, he gets into trouble, and Neytiri, a beautiful Na'vi female, saves his life. He is then taken in by her clan through a process involving many trials and tests. As Jake's relationship with Neytiri deepens, he learns to respect the Na'vi culture. He then faces the ultimate test as he leads the Na'vi in an epic battle that will decide the fate of an entire world.

Saldana has said that she pursued a role in *Avatar* because of the director, James Cameron. "He was why I got into movies," she revealed. "His female heroes—Ripley [from the *Alien* movies] and Sarah Connor [from the *Terminator* franchise]—showed me an actress can be an action hero." To prepare for the role of Neytiri, Saldana trained for six months, studying martial arts, archery, and horseback riding. She also had to learn the language of the Na'vi that was created for the movie. Because Neytiri is a computer-generated character, Saldana doesn't actually appear on screen in the movie. The film's innovative "motion capture technology for animation" means that all her movements, from ballet-like leaps to facial expressions, are translated into a cartoon version of herself. To accomplish this, Saldana and many of the other *Avatar* actors had to wear special bodysuits fitted with sensors as well as helmets laced with cameras. "It wasn't as easy as everybody thinks where you just show up and lend your voice and have these visual illustrators try to create a character out of it. Everything we did—95% of it—was translated onto the screen." To portray Neytiri, Saldana studied the movements of certain animals. "My character is very agile, a hunter and a warrior. We looked a lot at the feline kingdom for inspiration. And she's very playful, so we looked at dolphins."

> **“**
>
> *To portray Neytiri in* **Avatar,** *Saldana studied the movements of certain animals. "My character is very agile, a hunter and a warrior. We looked a lot at the feline kingdom for inspiration. And she's very playful, so we looked at dolphins."*
>
> **”**

Avatar was a runaway success with moviegoers and won 31 film industry awards, including three Oscars, while also being nominated for 53 additional awards. Critics, however, gave the film mixed reviews. "It's dazzling, engulfing, a techno-dream for the senses, but one that's likely to leave audiences at once amazed and unmoved," Ty Burr wrote in *Entertainment Weekly.* "[The use of 3D renders the whole world] heightened, popping, bolder than life.... It's the story and the characters that could have used another dimension or two." Writing in the *New York Times,* movie critic Manohla Dargis praised the film: "If the story of a paradise found and potentially lost feels resonant, it's because *Avatar* is as much about our Earth as the universe that Mr. Cameron has invented. But the movie's truer meaning is in the audacity of its filmmaking. Few films return us to the lost world of our first cinematic experiences, to that magical moment when movies really were bigger than life.... Movies rarely carry us away, few even try. What's often missing is awe,

Saldana as Neytiri, a fearless and beautiful warrior who is a member of Pandora's royal clan of Na'vi.

something Mr. Cameron has, after an absence from Hollywood, returned to the screen with a vengeance. He hasn't changed cinema, but with blue people and pink blooms he has confirmed its wonder."

Future Plans

Saldana has several projects lined up to follow her successes in *Star Trek* and *Avatar*. "I find myself looking for roles that are strong,"' she acknowledged. "I'm easily turned off from roles that are soccer moms or love interests. If you really want me to say no, tell me that I will be 'the chick in the flick.' I have an issue with that.... I don't feel that there are enough roles that resemble the American women nowadays in Hollywood. It's almost an insult when you read scripts and you see that the guy's the hero."

Saldana enjoys acting in science fiction movies because of the potential for strong female characters. However, she said, "I wish there were more genres in which women could have more opportunities to be presented as what we are. We're complex creatures, we're very intricate, we also have journeys. We can be the heroes and we can save everyone. We can also be vulnerable, and we can be saved as well, all in one person."

Saldana can be seen in the 2010 movie *Death at a Funeral*, a comedy about family mishaps, miscommunication, and mixups surrounding the funeral of the family's father. The story mixes the crazy behavior and unexpected problems of characters played by a large all-star cast led by Chris Rock and Martin Lawrence and also featuring Loretta Devine, Danny Glover, Regina

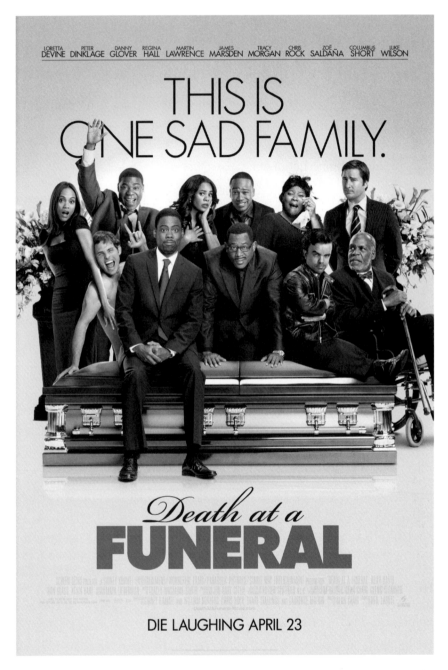

Saldana appeared with an all-star cast in the 2010 comedy Death at a Funeral.

Hall, Tracy Morgan and Luke Wilson. Saldana plays Elaine, a cousin who is badgered at the funeral by a persistent ex-boyfriend who demands that she break up with her current boyfriend and return to him. She also has a role in the 2010 movie *The Losers*, an adaptation of the DC-Vertigo comic book about members of a top-secret CIA team who plan revenge after they were left for dead on a dangerous mission. She plays Aisha, a blood-thirsty mercenary killer who thrives on close combat.

When planning her long-term career as an actor, Saldana hasn't been shy about acknowledging her dream of winning an Oscar some day. "I'm not going to be like, 'I just want to be known for my work,'" she declared. "No, I want that golden statue on my shelf. Whether it happens or not, it will not determine the kind of substance that I feel I contributed. But I want it.... Shoot for the stars and I'll settle for a cloud."

HOME AND FAMILY

Saldana lives with her boyfriend Keith Britton and divides her time between homes in New York City and Los Angeles. She has a dog named Calvin, a pit bull-pointer mix that she adopted from a shelter.

SELECTED CREDITS

Center Stage, 2000
Get Over It, 2001
Crossroads, 2002
Drumline, 2002
Pirates of the Caribbean: The Curse of the Black Pearl, 2003
The Terminal, 2004
Guess Who?, 2005
Star Trek, 2009
Avatar, 2009
The Losers, 2010
Death at a Funeral, 2010

HONORS AND AWARDS

Young Hollywood One to Watch Award (*Movieline* magazine): 2004, for her performance in *The Terminal*

FURTHER READING

Periodicals

Cosmopolitan, May 2009, p.104

Ebony, Mar. 2005
Entertainment Weekly, Aug. 21, 2009, p.88; Nov. 13, 2009, p.58; Jan. 29, 2010, p.24
Hispanic, June 2004
Interview, July 2004, p.32
Latina, May 2009; July 2009
US Weekly, Dec. 28, 2009, p.68
USA Today, Jan. 5, 2010, p.D2
Women's Health, May 2009

Online Articles

http://www.hollywoodtoday.net
(Hollywood Today, "*Avatar* Heroines, Zoë Saldana and Sigourney Weaver," Dec. 19, 2009)
http://www.people.com
(People, "*Avatar*'s Zoë Saldana Is Proud to Be a Geek," Dec. 21, 2009)
http://www.tvguide.com
(TV Guide, "Zoe Saldana, no date)
http://movies.yahoo.com
(Yahoo, "Zoe Saldana," no date)

ADDRESS

Zoë Saldana
International Creative Management
10250 Constellation Blvd.
Los Angeles, CA 90067

WORLD WIDE WEB SITES

http://www.zoesaldana.com
http://www.avatarmovie.com
http://www.startrekmovie.com
http://www.startrek.com

Caroll Spinney 1933-
American Puppeteer and Artist
Creator of Big Bird and Oscar the Grouch on
"Sesame Street"

BIRTH

Caroll Edwin Spinney was born on December 26, 1933, in Waltham, Massachusetts, a western suburb of Boston. He was the third and youngest son of Chester Spinney, who worked in a watch factory, and Margaret Spinney, who had left her home in England as a young girl to work in North America. She was an aspiring fashion illustrator and designer who put aside her career to focus on raising her sons, David,

Donald, and Caroll, who was so named because he barely missed being born on Christmas.

YOUTH

Spinney grew up in Acton, Massachusetts, a rural area west of Boston. He was so small as a child that he was nicknamed "Pee Wee" in first and second grade and felt self-conscious about his size. He would later bring these emotions from childhood to his most famous character, "Big Bird gets frustrated and a little insecure, because I certainly was. I was the small kid in the neighborhood and I was pushed around a lot," he remembered. "I always wanted people to like me, because I wasn't cool." In fact, he has said he was shy. "If the word 'nerd' existed back then, that's what I would've been considered—even though I don't like that word." He especially loved comics and drawing: "I drew all the time. If it was cold weather, when [I] came in from playing or sliding in the winter, I would then start drawing on my comic books."

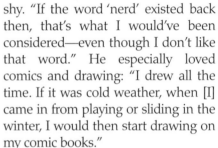

"Big Bird gets frustrated and a little insecure, because I certainly was," Spinney remembered. "I was the small kid in the neighborhood and I was pushed around a lot. I always wanted people to like me, because I wasn't cool."

Spinney was five years old when he first saw a puppet show, put on by some college students at a neighbor's day care. He enjoyed it so much he bought a monkey puppet at a rummage sale for a nickel and used a stuffed flannel snake his mother had made him as another prop. By age eight, he had built a puppet theater out of old crates and performed a show in his family's barn. He charged his neighbors and friends two cents a ticket, and after 20 minutes "everybody went away smiling," he recalled. "I already wanted to be a cartoonist when I grew up. After this show, I decided that I would also become a puppeteer." For a shy person who liked performing, puppetry made sense. When he stayed behind the curtain, he didn't feel awkward at all. "As a puppeteer you can hide whatever you are at the moment and be only what they see," he said. "And you could get the adults to laugh." For Spinney's next Christmas, his mother and his brother Donald created a Punch-and-Judy puppet theater with a complete set of puppets to go along with it. Spinney's mother also wrote scripts for her son's puppet shows.

Spinney was also interested in television, a new invention that was spreading across the country after World War II. He first saw a TV at the 1940

World's Fair. "I remember looking at it and thinking—the idea just came to me—a television looks a lot like a puppet theater. I wanted to do puppets on television. I hadn't even seen it done, but I knew that it could be." When TV first came to the Boston area in 1947 and the neighborhood doctor purchased a set, Spinney visited the house to see what was on. One of the children's programs he saw had a puppet skit that he knew he could have performed much better. It gave him confidence that he could turn his love of puppetry into a successful career. "I decided some day I'm going to be on the best TV kids' show," he recalled.

EDUCATION

In the early 1950s, Spinney graduated from Acton High School, where a teacher supported his career goal of becoming a puppeteer. Although his father wanted him to start working right away, Spinney entered the Art Institute of Boston's College of Art and Design. There he studied illustration and commercial art, thinking it would be a practical major. He supported himself by performing puppet shows at birthday parties and holiday gatherings. He interrupted his studies to serve in the U.S. Air Force for four years, but after his service he returned to school and completed his degree in the late 1950s.

When Spinney learned how to keep his live audience entertained for 45 minutes, he was hooked. "Once I started performing live for the camera," he noted, "I knew that was what I wanted to do."

CAREER HIGHLIGHTS

Starting His First Television Show

When Spinney enlisted in the Air Force, he managed to pass a draftsman's exam and was stationed at a base in Las Vegas, Nevada. There he drew technical instructional charts and training aids such as a poster instructing "How to Bomb and Strafe." Because the weather in Las Vegas was so hot, Spinney performed his Air Force duties during the earliest part of the day, leaving his afternoons free. He used his spare time to put on puppet shows for local groups, and one such performance led to a contact with local television station KLAS. They hired him to draw advertising cards, then gave him time for his own children's program. "The Rascal Rabbit Show," using a white rabbit puppet his mother had made for him, debuted on KLAS-TV in 1955. When Spinney learned how to keep his live audience entertained for 45 minutes, he was hooked. "Once I started performing live for the

Spinney's characters from "Sesame Street": Big Bird and Oscar the Grouch.

camera," he noted, "I knew that was what I wanted to do." The show only lasted a couple of months, because the Air Force soon ordered him to transfer to Bitburg, Germany. He found a way to express himself there as well, contributing a comic strip to the local armed service newspaper.

When Spinney left the Air Force in 1957, he got an interview with the Walt Disney Company, which produced many of his favorite cartoons. Their offer to hire him as an animator would have fulfilled a long-time ambition, but the pay was so dismal he decided to return to Boston to finish his degree. While there he created animations for commercials and collaborated on the "Crazy Crayon" cartoon series. He discovered that creating animation wasn't as satisfying as performing for a live audience. "The only trouble with art is that it's very lonely. I don't get any applause until later," he remarked. In 1958, he auditioned for a Boston television station that was looking to create a new children's program. Although he didn't get the job, they called him later and asked if he would contribute to a television series for children that would air during the summer season. He soon was starring with singer Judy Valentine in "The Judy and Goggle Show," which was set inside a spaceship and included Goggle, his yellow bird puppet with "goggle" eyes. Although the show earned excellent ratings for its time slot, the station didn't have room in its schedule to broadcast it after the summer.

Instead, the same Boston station offered Spinney a job performing on "Bozo's Big Top," a successful children's show that franchised the character of Bozo the Clown to local stations around the United States. Starting in 1959, Spinney performed with hand puppets and acted in costume as several characters. These included Grandma Nellie, Bozo's clown grandmother; Kookie, a boxing kangaroo; and Mr. Lion, the "fastest draw alive." For the Mr. Lion segment, the costumed Spinney would write down a child's name and turn it into an animal drawing in less than 30 seconds. Although his first drawing challenge was on the spur of the moment, it became a regular feature of the show. Much of the show was unscripted. "We kind of made it up as we went along," he later remembered. "We had no writers. Sometimes it was quite funny. I wish I had tapes of it, because I think some of it must have been really bad." For most of his run on "Bozo's Big Top" Spinney performed in front of a live audience three days a week, but there was still something unsatisfactory about the job. "While what I was doing paid pretty well," he said, "it did not make me feel I had ever done anything really important."

That changed after a performance at the 1969 Puppeteers of America convention. Spinney had been experimenting with combining animation and puppetry, performing his characters against a screen that used film as moving scenery. For the convention, he built an elaborate stage and chore-

> **"**
>
> *Spinney was excited about the prospect of working with Jim Henson, the creator of the Muppets. "I was somewhat in awe of him. The live shows I'd seen him put on—the ideas, the puppets, and the performances—were incredible.... When I saw Jim's commercials and TV appearances, I realized just how well puppets and television could be done."*
>
> **"**

ographed a show that synchronized music, animation, and live performance of his cat puppet, Picklepuss, which he brought from "Bozo." On the day of the show, however, a misplaced spotlight hid the animated scenery and ruined the program. While waiting for someone to fix the light, Spinney improvised with Picklepuss and some shadow puppets. "My character, Picklepuss, in his struggles to save the day, ended up being funnier than my material," Spinney remembered. In the audience that day was Jim Henson, the legendary creator of the Muppets who was already nationally famous for his performances on "The Ed Sullivan Show." Henson invited Spinney to New York to talk about a job on a new children's program. Spinney was excited about the prospect of working with Henson. "I was somewhat in awe of him. The live shows I'd seen him put on—the ideas, the puppets, and the performances—were incredible.... When I saw Jim's commercials and TV appearances, I realized just how well puppets and television could be done."

Moving to "Sesame Street"

When Spinney met with Henson, he learned the Muppets would be working on a children's show for the Public Broadcasting System (PBS) called "Sesame Street." Its goal was to use the latest research about how children learn to create a television show that would teach them such simple concepts as counting and the alphabet. Henson was looking for a puppeteer to take two roles: a large, goofy bird and a grouchy character named Oscar. "I wondered what the Bird and Oscar would actually do, as there were no scripts available at this point," Spinney recalled. "I had no idea how they would fit in the show, or what voices I would use. Still, I was confident I could learn. I *had* to do this! I was being asked to work for someone who, in my mind, was the greatest puppeteer in history. This show *had* to work." Although it meant a large pay cut and a commute from Boston to New York City, Spinney agreed to join the show.

"Sesame Street" first aired in fall 1969, with Spinney's character of Big Bird only appearing for one or two minutes each episode. Henson originally pictured the character as a goofy country bumpkin who kept running into things. "He didn't have a clue about anything, and it seemed that he had no real purpose on the show except as a comic diversion," Spinney noted. "Certainly, he had no educational value." That changed when Spinney read a script that called for Big Bird to be upset because he couldn't join kids at day care. The puppeteer thought it sounded creepy for a goofy adult to want to go to day care, so "I said, 'Let's make sure the audience knows that he's a kid.' That way he could go to day care and play with the other kids." It also meant that Big Bird could learn things along with the audience. After playing the scene where Big Bird throws a tantrum because he can't join other kids at day care, the puppeteer remarked, "it felt very natural, and I knew that suddenly I had a real, human, complex character to work with. He was the too-big kid, much as I had been the too-little kid when I was his age."

The look of the Big Bird puppet also evolved with Spinney's feedback. When the puppeteer first began performing Big Bird, he couldn't see out of the costume. The first time he saw his performance on a monitor, he remembered, "I was shocked when I saw ... how much his head was flailing

*"Sesame Street" hosts Gordon (Matt Robinson), Mr. Hooper (Will Lee), Susan
(Loretta Lee), and Bob (Bob McGrath) stand with Big Bird on the set of the TV
series in about 1969.*

around and his feathers were all put on inverted so that the bottoms, the
underside of the feathers were showing." The Muppet designers adapted
the puppet by putting feathers with the shiny sides up, and reshaping his
head. Eventually the puppet reached eight feet two inches tall, close to the

159

limit that the five-foot ten-inch Spinney could reach. During that second year, Henson also rigged a monitor for him inside the suit, so Spinney could see what the camera was seeing and make sure Big Bird was looking in the right direction.

Because Spinney worked the controls of Big Bird's head with his hand, the suit was considered a "walkabout" puppet, not a costume. Spinney wore costume pants for Big Bird's legs, then raised his right hand above his head to work Big Bird's mouth. His left hand went in Big Bird's left wing, and a wire let him move the right wing in the opposite direction of the left. Because Big Bird's head weighed more than four pounds, Spinney couldn't stay in the suit much more than 10 minutes. Despite being limited to brief segments, Big Bird quickly became the most popular character on the show. Spinney received many fan letters addressed to Big Bird inviting him to come over and play.

> ——— " ———
>
> *Spinney was gratified when he saw his "Sesame Street" characters on a children's book cover along with several Disney characters. "What satisfaction I felt! Some of the most magical moments of my childhood were watching Disney cartoons," he recalled. "Seeing my characters dancing with Bugs and Mickey told me that I shared in those magic moments for other children. It hadn't hit me before. Now I knew that I had gotten to where I wanted to be."*
>
> ——— " ———

Spinney's other character for "Sesame Street," Oscar the Grouch, required a completely different approach. The puppeteer knew Oscar was supposed to live in a trash can, but he wasn't sure exactly how to flesh out the character. A chance encounter provided inspiration. "I was going to meet Jim to do a run-through on Oscar for the first time," Spinney recalled. "I was supposed to have a voice ready, and still couldn't decide when I got into a cab and the driver said, 'Where to, Mac?'" While the driver colorfully complained about the local mayor, the puppeteer added, "I just kept saying to myself, 'Where to, Mac? Where to, Mac?' and I realized that sounded just right." He used that voice on his first run-through with the puppet, having Oscar tell Jim Henson, "Get away from my trash can!" "That'll do nicely," Henson told Spinney, and the gruff but lovable Oscar became a regular on the show.

When in character Spinney often works with children, as in this encounter between Big Bird and students from the Overbrook School for the Blind.

Becoming a Television Pioneer

During its first season, "Sesame Street" was immediately hailed as one of the best children's programs ever, winning a Peabody Award and three Emmys—the first of more than 100 Emmys the show has won during its

161

first 40 years. "I can't imagine we were acclaimed, it was so crude and amateurish," Spinney remembered. "But compared to what was on TV at the time as far as content, we were way ahead of them right from the start. Because this was the only show that really studied how to teach children." Still, the puppeteer almost left after the first year finished filming. He spent his summer performing on "Bozo's Big Top" in Boston and the station offered him his own "Picklepuss" show. Spinney decided to think it over for a month, but soon realized he was working in a dream job, reaching a larger audience than he could have imagined as a child. In November 1970 Big Bird was on the cover of *Time* magazine, and later Spinney saw his "Sesame Street" characters on a children's book cover along with several Disney characters and Bugs Bunny. "There were *my* characters, perfectly cartooned, dancing with my favorite cartoon characters from childhood," he recalled. "What satisfaction I felt! Some of the most magical moments of my childhood were watching Disney cartoons. Seeing my characters dancing with Bugs and Mickey told me that I shared in those magic moments for other children. It hadn't hit me before. Now I knew that I had gotten to where I wanted to be."

During the 1970s and 1980s, Spinney earned four Emmy Awards for individual performance and two Grammy Awards for contributing to the best children's recording of the year. He also received invitations for Big Bird and Oscar to guest star on other TV shows. He appeared on several variety shows and became a frequent guest of the game show "Hollywood Squares," eventually appearing on more than 140 episodes. Spinney's characters were also invited to appear at many public events. He made an appearance in 1971 with the Boston Pops, with Big Bird conducting the orchestra. This led to a series of tours in which Spinney's Big Bird would conduct a musical program; Spinney would perform in 10-minute segments, then go backstage to rest and take oxygen. He conducted groups across the U.S., Canada, and Australia, until the travel and effort became too exhausting. He also became a frequent visitor at the White House, making his first trip in 1971 at the invitation of First Lady Patricia Nixon and meeting every First Lady since then. Performing as Oscar, he shared a stage with Prince Charles of Britain.

Spinney's frequent television appearances led to many travel opportunities as well. In 1979 comedian Bob Hope invited him to join a special taped in China. The communist nation had long been closed to outsiders and had only recently opened itself to political and cultural exchanges with the United States. While taping "Bob Hope on the Road of China," Spinney's Big Bird did a song and dance number with Hope and also got a chance to entertain the local children. They were fascinated with Big Bird despite the language difference, and Spinney returned home, determined to explore the country further. He came up with the idea of having Big Bird discover he is related to the Phoenix of China, a legendary bird, and travel there to find her. The result was the 1983 program "Big Bird in China," which was a hit both in the United States and China.

Spinney also appeared in several movies as both Big Bird and Oscar, most notably taking a starring role in the 1985 feature *Follow That Bird*. The film begins with a social worker noticing that Big Bird doesn't live with other birds and sending him to Illinois to live with a family of dodos. His new family has no imagination and Big Bird misses his friends, so he decides to walk to New York City to get back to Sesame Street. At the same time, his Sesame Street friends go in search of the missing Bird, and Big Bird and his friends have many adventures along the way. While celebrity cameos livened up the film, "the person who seems to hold the movie together is Caroll Spinney, the Muppeteer who, under all those yellow feathers, plays the bird we would follow anywhere," remarked Jay Boyar, a critic for the *Orlando Sentinel*.

Creating a Lasting Legacy

Although Spinney has worked on "Sesame Street" for more than 40 years, one episode in particular stands out in his mind. Actor Will Lee, who had played shopkeeper Mr. Hooper since the first season, died in late 1982 from a heart attack. The

"'Sesame Street,' I've come to realize, is a big place," Spinney said. *"Sure, some characters become more popular than others for periods of time, but the show has always been a group effort in the service of our mission. Sharing and cooperation, getting along with others, and recognizing one another's strengths are some of our most important social messages, after all."*

show's producers debated how to address the actor's departure and considered having the character retire. Finally they decided to deal with the issue of death head on. When Big Bird wants to give Mr. Hooper a portrait he drew, the adults on Sesame Street have to explain that death means Mr. Hooper will never be coming back. "When the scene ended, all the actors in the cast had genuine tears in their eyes," Spinney recalled. "We used the first take, because it was so real. I think this scene was the best one we did in all the … years of 'Sesame Street.' It was our tribute to Will Lee." Big

Big Bird reads to children on "Sesame Street."

Bird's drawing of Mr. Hooper—which the puppeteer drew himself—still remains a part of the set in Big Bird's nest.

Over 40 years, there have been many changes at "Sesame Street." Producers changed the format to include longer stories when research showed young viewers could follow them, and they made other adjustments as the average audience member became younger. Financial issues meant the number of episodes per season shrank from over 100 the first season to 26 in season 40. New characters came to the show; one in particular, a little red Muppet named Elmo, became even more popular than Big Bird. Spinney welcomed the changes as a chance to keep teaching kids. "'Sesame Street,' I've come to realize, is a big place," he said. "Sure, some characters become more popular than others for periods of time, but the show has always been a group effort in the service of our mission. Sharing and cooperation, getting along with others, and recognizing one another's strengths are some of our most important social messages, after all."

Even grouchy Oscar has a lot to teach children, according to his puppeteer: "I think [he] teaches kids that it takes all kinds in the world." Spinney said he finds Oscar a refreshing change after being sweet-natured Big Bird all day, and he insisted that Oscar is "not a villain, not horrible, … and although he can be rude and mean, he fundamentally has got a heart of gold." He explained that Oscar is a "perfectionist" who's passionate about trash. "He's into his thing, he's often alone, and when somebody intrudes on him, naturally he gets grouchy." If Spinney reads a script where Oscar crosses the line of being too rude, he will ask for changes. "Honestly, I'm often surprised at what he's going to say, but my mother and father were very funny and that's why it comes easy for me, or for the puppet."

After performing as Big Bird and Oscar for over 40 years, Spinney revealed that "working the puppet has become something like touch typing. I don't have to think about it too much, and I can concentrate on expressing what Big Bird is thinking and feeling. I didn't create the puppet, and I don't write the scripts, but I guess what I do is bring Big Bird his soul.… He's the child that I wanted to be, the kind of person I think we all should be."

Spending more than half his life playing Big Bird and Oscar has earned Spinney many accolades. In 2000, the Library of Congress gave him the Living Legend Award for his work as Big Bird, while his television peers voted him a Lifetime Achievement Emmy Award in 2006. (He earned his fifth Emmy for individual performance the following year.) While he finds these kinds of awards satisfying, the puppeteer is most gratified by

The cast of "Sesame Street" on its 40th anniversary.

the response he gets from the public. When Spinney went on a book tour for his 2003 memoir *The Wisdom of Big Bird,* he had a chance to meet many fans who might otherwise not recognize him. "I've talked to dozens of people on this tour who say, 'You have no idea how important you were to our family,'" he recalled. "I don't know how I could have been so fortunate."

After performing as Big Bird and Oscar for over 40 years, Spinney revealed that "working the puppet has become something like touch typing. I don't have to think about it too much, and I can concentrate on expressing what Big Bird is thinking and feeling. I didn't create the puppet, and I don't write the scripts, but I guess what I do is bring Big Bird his soul.… He's the child that I wanted to be, the kind of person I think we all should be." Although he has been limited to two characters for a lengthy time, he said he never gets bored with the work. "There's a huge dramatic range," he remarked. "I've gone from blubbering tears to wild happiness. It's very satisfying." Besides, he added, "even though the Bird appears very birdlike and does birdy things like live in a nest, he really is as human as anyone on the show." Spinney's goal is to keep exploring his characters' humanity as long as he is physically able to do so. "When I no longer can hold that bird's head up where it belongs, then I guess I'll have to say, 'Hasta la vista,'" he commented. "It's just so much of a joy to do it. It's physically demanding, which keeps me in good shape. I'm not one who adores doing exercise, but the last thing I want to do at this point is retire."

MARRIAGE AND FAMILY

Spinney married his first wife, Janice, sometime in the 1960s. They had three children, Jessica, Melissa, and Benjamin, and divorced in 1971. Spinney met his second wife, Debra Jean Gilroy, at the Children's Television Workshop, where she worked as a secretary. They married in 1979 and moved to a country home in Woodstock, Connecticut. The couple also has a studio apartment in New York City, where they spend time during the shooting season of "Sesame Street."

HOBBIES AND OTHER INTERESTS

Throughout his years working as puppeteer, Spinney has continued working as an artist. He regularly draws cartoons, and when he can find the time he creates acrylic paintings, often featuring the character of Big Bird. Some of his works are for sale as prints or originals, and some he has donated to benefit charities.

SELECTED CREDITS

Television Series and Specials

"Bozo's Big Top," 1959-69
"Sesame Street," 1969-
"Hollywood Squares," 1976-80, 2001
"Christmas Eve on Sesame Street," 1978
"Bob Hope on the Road of China," 1979
"Big Bird in China," 1983
"Big Bird Brings Spring to Sesame Street," 1987
"A Muppet Family Christmas," 1987
"Big Bird in Japan," 1988
"Big Bird's Birthday or Let Me Eat Cake," 1991
"Elmo Saves Christmas," 1996

Films

The Muppet Movie, 1979
The Great Muppet Caper, 1981
Follow That Bird, 1985
The Adventures of Elmo in Grouchland, 1999

Books

How to Be a Grouch, 1976 (as Oscar the Grouch; author and illustrator)
The Wisdom of Big Bird (and the Dark Genius of Oscar the Grouch): Lessons from a Life in Feathers, 2003 (with J. Mulligan)

Recordings

Big Bird Sings!, 1973
Big Bird Leads the Band, 1977
Bounce along with Big Bird, 1985
Bird Is the Word!: Big Bird's Favorite Songs, 1995
Sesame Street: Oscar's Trashy Songs, 1997
A Sesame Street Christmas, 2002

HONORS AND AWARDS

Grammy Award for Best Recording for Children (The Recording Academy): two awards for "Sesame Street" recordings
Emmy Award (National Academy of Television Arts and Sciences): 1974, 1976, and 1979, Outstanding Individual Achievement in Children's Programming (with others), 1984, Special Classification of Outstanding Individual Achievement—Performers, and 2007, Outstanding Performer in a Children's Series (with Kevin Clash), all for "Sesame Street"
Hollywood Walk of Fame: 1994 (as Big Bird)
Living Legend Award (Library of Congress): 2000
Legacy for Children Award (Children's Discovery Museum): 2003
James Keller Award (The Christopher Awards, Inc): 2004
Emmy Award (National Academy of Television Arts and Sciences): 2006, Lifetime Achievement Award

FURTHER READING

Books

Davis, Michael. *Street Gang: The Complete History of Sesame Street,* 2008
Spinney, Caroll, with J. Mulligan. *The Wisdom of Big Bird (and the Dark Genius of Oscar the Grouch): Lessons from a Life in Feathers,* 2003

Periodicals

Atlanta Journal-Constitution, May 9, 2003, p.E6
Chicago Tribune, Nov. 14, 1989
Current Biography, 1999
Daily Variety, Mar. 17, 2006, p.A1
Los Angeles Times, Sep. 15, 1991, p.36; May 21, 2003
New York Times, Nov. 11, 1998
New Yorker, Nov. 9. 2009
Orlando Sentinel, Aug. 4, 1985, p.F1
People Weekly, Dec. 4, 2000, p.115
Television Quarterly, Fall 2006, p.61

Washington Post, June 22, 2008, p.A7
Winston-Salem Journal, Nov. 16, 1998, p.D1

Online Articles

http://www.emmytvlegends.org
   (Archive of American Television, "Caroll Spinney—Archive Interview,"
   May 12, 2001)
http://today.msnbc.msn.com/id/25193936
   (MSNBC, "As Big Bird, Caroll Spinney Loves Every Feather," June 16,
   2008)
http://www.npr.org
   (National Public Radio, "A Life Inside Big Bird," May 5, 2003)
http://www.npr.org
   (National Public Radio, "Voice of Big Bird, Oscar Wins Lifetime Award,"
   Apr. 27, 2006)
http://artsbeat.blogs.nytimes.com/2009/11/09/big-bird-responds
   (New York Times, "Big Bird Responds," Nov. 11, 2009)
http://www.nytimes.com
   (New York Times, "Public Lives: 30 Happy Years as an 8-Foot Tall Yellow
   Bird," Nov. 11, 1998)
http://www.topics.nytimes.com
   (New York Times, "Sesame Street," multiple articles, various dates)
http://content.usatoday.com/topics/topic/Caroll+Spinney
   (USA Today, "Caroll Spinney," multiple articles, various dates)

ADDRESS

Caroll Spinney
Sesame Workshop
One Lincoln Plaza
New York, NY 10023

WORLD WIDE WEB SITES

http://www.carollspinney.com
http://www.sesamestreet.org/onair/cast

Photo and Illustration Credits

Front Cover Photos: Justin Bieber: Pamela Littky/© 2009 Universal Music Group; Drew Brees: AP Photos/Ben Liebenberg; Ursula Burns: Nik Rocklin/Courtesy of Xerox Corporation; Zoë Saldana: Movie: AVATAR™ and WETA/© 2009 Twentieth Century Fox Film Corporation. All rights reserved.

Justin Bieber/Photos: Pamela Littky/© 2010 Universal Music Group (p. 9); Pamela Littky/© 2009 Universal Music Group (p. 12); Giulio Marcocchi/Sipa Press/KIDS_gm .177/0903291339 via Newscom (p. 14); Kevin Winter/Courtesy of Nickelodeon 2010 Kids' Choice Awards (p. 16); CD: MY WORLD. Island Records/© 2010 Universal Music Group (p. 18).

Drew Brees/Photos: AP Photo/Eric Gay (p. 21); Courtesy Purdue University Sports Information (p. 24); AP Photo/Paul Spinelli (p. 26); AP Photo/Eric Gay (p. 29); John Gress/Reuters/Landov (p. 31); Scott Clarke/ESPN (p. 33); AP Photo/Kevin Terrell (p. 34).

Ursula Burns/Photos: Lonnie Major/Courtesy of Xerox Corporation (p. 39); Newscom (p. 42); Courtesy of Xerox Corporation (p. 45); Stephanie Kuykendal/Bloomberg via Getty Images (p. 47); Courtesy of Xerox Corporation (p. 48).

Gustavo Dudamel/Photos: Mathais Bothor/Deutsche Grammophon/Courtesy Thirteen/WNET New York/PBS (p. 53); Chris Christodoulou/Courtesy Thirteen/WNET New York/PBS (p. 55); Deutsche Grammophon/UMD/Universal Music Group (p. 58); John Bohn/Boston Globe/Landov (p. 61); Mathew Imaging/Courtesy Thirteen/WNET New York/PBS (p. 62); AP Photo/Mark J. Terrill (p. 64).

Tavi Gevinson/Photos: Astrid Stawiarz/Getty Images (p. 69); Heather Charles/MCT/Landov (p. 72); Patrick Kovarik/AFP/Getty Images (p. 75); AP Photo/Jennifer Graylock (p. 77).

LeBron James/Photos: Marc Serota/Getty Images (p. 81); Book: SHOOTING STARS (2009, The Penguin Press) by LeBron James and Buzz Bissinger. Copyright © LeBron James. All rights reserved. Photo by Patty Burdon. Jacket Design by Darren Haggar. (p. 83); Bob Leverone/TSN/Icon SMI/via Newscom (p. 86); AP Photo/Mark Duncan (p. 89); AP Photo/Duane Burleson (p. 91); Adam Hunger/Reuters/Landov (p. 94); AP Photo/Phil Long (p. 97).

Taylor Lautner/Photos: Kevin Winter/Getty Images for KCA (p. 101); DVD: THE ADVENTURES OF SHARKBOY AND LAVAGIRL © Buena Vista Home Entertainment, Inc. (p. 104); Movie: THE TWILIGHT SAGA: NEW MOON. Kimberley

Cumulative Names Index

This cumulative index includes the names of all individuals profiled in *Biography Today* since the debut of the series in 1992.

For cumulative general, places of birth, and birthday indexes, please see biographytoday.com.

For cumulative general, places of birth, and birthday indexes, please see biographytoday.com.

For cumulative general, places of birth, and birthday indexes, please see biographytoday.com.

179

For cumulative general, places of birth, and birthday indexes, please see biographytoday.com.

For cumulative general, places of birth, and birthday indexes, please see biographytoday.com.

For cumulative general, places of birth, and birthday indexes, please see biographytoday.com.

For cumulative general, places of birth, and birthday indexes, please see biographytoday.com.

For cumulative general, places of birth, and birthday indexes, please see biographytoday.com.

189

Biography Today

General Series

For ages 9 and above

Biography Today **General Series** includes a unique combination of current biographical profiles that teachers and librarians — and the readers themselves — tell us are most appealing. The **General Series** is available as a 3-issue subscription; hardcover annual cumulation; or subscription plus cumulation.

Within the **General Series**, your readers will find a variety of sketches about:

- Authors
- Musicians
- Political leaders
- Sports figures
- Movie actresses & actors
- Cartoonists
- Scientists
- Astronauts
- TV personalities
- and the movers & shakers in many other fields!

"*Biography Today* will be useful in elementary and middle school libraries and in public library children's collections where there is a need for biographies of current personalities. High schools serving reluctant readers may also want to consider a subscription."
— *Booklist*, American Library Association

"Highly recommended for the young adult audience. Readers will delight in the accessible, energetic, tell-all style; teachers, librarians, and parents will welcome the clever format [and] intelligent and informative text. It should prove especially useful in motivating 'reluctant' readers or literate nonreaders."
— *MultiCultural Review*

"Written in a friendly, almost chatty tone, the profiles offer quick, objective information. While coverage of current figures makes *Biography Today* a useful reference tool, an appealing format and wide scope make it a fun resource to browse." — *School Library Journal*

"The best source for current information at a level kids can understand."
— Kelly Bryant, School Librarian, Carlton, OR

"Easy for kids to read. We love it! Don't want to be without it."
— Lynn McWhirter, School Librarian, Rockford, IL

ONE-YEAR SUBSCRIPTION

- 3 softcover issues, 6" x 9"
- Published in January, April, and September
- 1-year subscription, list price $66.
  School and library price $64
- 150 pages per issue
- 10 profiles per issue
- Contact sources for additional information
- Cumulative Names Index

HARDBOUND ANNUAL CUMULATION

- Sturdy 6" x 9" hardbound volume
- Published in December
- List price $73. **School and library price $66 per volume**
- 450 pages per volume
- 30 profiles — includes all profiles found in softcover issues for that calendar year
- Cumulative General Index, Places of Birth Index, and Birthday Index

SUBSCRIPTION AND CUMULATION COMBINATION

- $110 for 3 softcover issues plus the hardbound volume

For Cumulative General, Places of Birth, and Birthday Indexes, please see www.biographytoday.com.